PATIOS &
WALKWAYS
IDEA BOOK

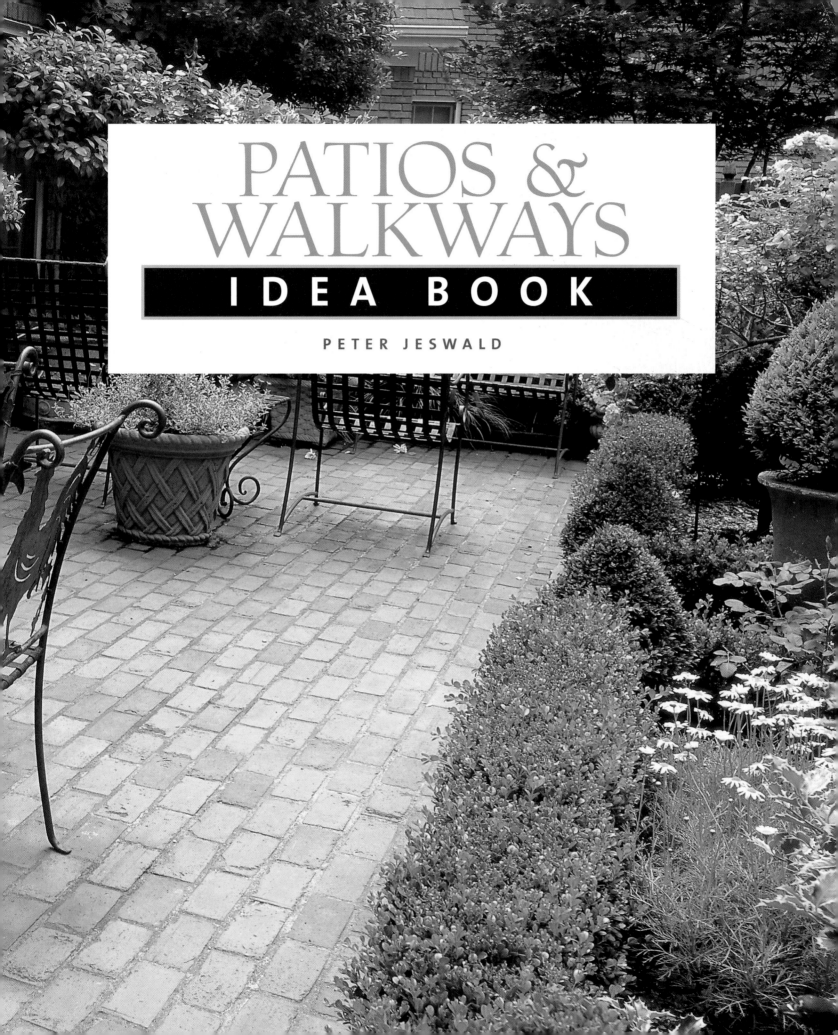

PATIOS & WALKWAYS
IDEA BOOK

PETER JESWALD

The Taunton Press, Inc., 63 South Main Street, PO Box 5506, Newtown, CT 06470-5506
e-mail: tp@taunton.com

Interior layout: Viewtistic Creative Partners
Illustrator: Christine Erikson
Copyeditor: Tammalene Mitman
Front cover photographers: (top row, left to right) ©Steve Vierra, © Lee Anne White,
© Lisa Romerein, ©www.carolynbates.com; (middle row, left to right) ©Anne Gummerson,
©Saxon Holt, ©Mark Lohman, ©Tria Giovan; (bottom row, left to right) ©Lee Anne White,
©Lisa Romerein, ©Jessie Walker, ©Mark Lohman
Back cover photographers: (top) ©Lisa Romerein; (bottom row, left to right) ©Mark Lohman,
©Mark Lohman, ©Chipper Hatter

Library of Congress Cataloging-in-Publication Data
Jeswald, Peter.
  Patios & walkways idea book
    p. cm.
  ISBN 978-1-56158-936-4
  1. Patios--Design and construction--Amateurs' manuals. I. Title. II. Title: Patios & walkways idea book.

TH4970.J48 2007
728'.93--dc22

                    2007018135

Printed in the United States of America
10 9 8 7 6 5

The following manufacturers/names appearing in *Patios & Walkways Idea Book* are trademarks: AIBD®,
American Institute of Architects®, American Society of Landscape Architects®, APLD®, Better Homes
and Gardens®, Big Wheels®, Energy Star®, Fine Gardening®, Garden Deck and Landscape®, Interlocking Concrete Paver Institute®, Master Landscape Pro™, Master Pools Guild™, National Association of the
Remodeling Industry®, National Pool and Spa Institute®, Punch! Software®, Storey®, Yardiac®

Acknowledgments

I would to thank Carolyn Mandarano, senior editor at Taunton Press, who continues to be a pleasure to work with, once again demonstrating her experience, expertise, and collaborative working style.

I thank the following people for taking time out of their busy schedules to answer my questions and share their insights: Ted Corvey, paver business director, Pine Hall Brick, Winston-Salem, North Carolina; Larry Nicolai, senior vice president, Ideal Concrete Block Company, Inc., Westford, Massachusetts; Walter Cudnohufsky, Walter Cudnohufsky Associates, Inc., Ashfield, Massachusetts; Beth Foote, manager, and the staff at Cook Builders' Supply, Easthampton, Massachusetts; and Mickey Grybko, sales manager, Amherst Farmers Supply, Amherst, Massachusetts.

Contents

Introduction

During the past several years a long-simmering trend has become a bona fide craze: The All-American yard has been transformed from a dull maintenance hog into valuable living space. Homeowners everywhere—in warm climates or cold—are realizing that the outdoors can be just as much a part of their homes as the indoors. Moving activities from the house into the yard—in effect, bringing some of the indoors outside—is blurring the distinction between the two. Patios are at the forefront of this growing phenomenon and often top landscape-construction wish lists.

One driving force behind the resurgent interest in patios is the development of numerous and attractive building material options. Brick and concrete pavers have benefited from advances in manufacturing techniques and are produced in an almost endless array of patterns and colors. Many types and shapes of stone, with its timeless quality and unmatched durability, can be purchased at local masonry supply yards and garden centers. New preservative treatments have made rot-resistant, pressure-treated wood safer to use. And a new family of materials made with recycled products makes building in the environment safer—for the environment.

One of the hallmarks of indoor living—comfort—also has found its way outside. Sitting on a patio should, and can, be every bit as comfortable as lounging in a living room. Recognizing the growing popularity of outdoor living, manufacturers are paying more attention to details, constructing more durable furniture, and creating styles that mimic indoor pieces. While cast iron and wood furniture still have their place, pieces made of lightweight extruded aluminum account for most of the outdoor furniture sold. In addition, colorful fabrics that can stand up to the elements now cover cushions and pillows.

More and more of the creature comforts that not too long ago were for indoor use only have found their way into backyards. Kitchen appliances such as refrigerators and beverage coolers, stereo systems, and sophisticated lighting are now available for outdoor use. Perhaps the most telling example is the television. TVs built with all-weather construction that can stand up to rain, dirt, and extreme temperatures can now be used to create a patio TV room.

Patios & Walkways Idea Book introduces you to this new and improved world of outdoor living. With hundreds of photographs to inspire you and solid information to guide you through the planning process, *Patios & Walkways Idea Book* is an excellent companion and valuable resource, whether you're planning a small patio or a complete backyard makeover.

Creating Outdoor Living Spaces

THE LAND AROUND YOUR HOME IS MUCH MORE than just a yard. It's a valuable resource that can enlarge your home's living space, enhance quality of life, and increase the value of your property. To make the most of this space, reframe the way you think about the outdoors. Houses don't have to be islands surrounded by seas of grass. Instead of "yard" or "lawn," think "landscape," where your home expands and blends seamlessly into its surroundings.

Patios and walkways are an important part of any home's landscape. Patios can create outdoor "rooms" for virtually every type of family activity— cooking, dining, playing—or they can be private spaces where you escape the household hubbub, put your feet up, and relax. Walkways connect your home to the outdoors and link together the different parts of your landscape. Whether a broad brick walk to the front door or a stepping-stone path to a secret garden, walkways direct traffic and make it easier to get around.

Other elements, such as stairs, walls, and overhead structures, go hand-in-hand with patios and walkways. Sometimes such elements are needed to deal with challenges like slopes and level changes; other times they're used to define and separate one space from another.

◄ PLACED ON THE NORTH SIDE OF THE HOME, this patio extends away from the shadows to reach the sunny portion of the yard. To make sure the entire family will enjoy outdoor living, the patio is set with two dining tables, one for adults and one for children.

Variations on a Patio

ONE OF THE REASONS PATIOS are so popular is because of their connection with earth. The land around a home is not always level, though, and that can present challenges when designing and building a patio. However, unless the land is exceptionally steep or the first floor of a home is very high above the ground, most of these challenges can be overcome. In fact, patios don't fall neatly into a single type, so one way to categorize them is by the construction method used to accommodate the idiosyncrasies of the landscape.

▲ THE STONE WALLS THAT BORDER THIS PATIO form beds for lush plantings, while the water feature adds to the tropical feel. The same type of flagstones that cover the patio also top the walls, bringing consistency to the space.

◄ SHELTERED UNDER A GENEROUS OVERHANG and positioned off to one side of the patio, this conversation grouping is the perfect place to while away the summer hours. The tight joints of the 4-in. by 8-in. pavers provide solid footing for the metal furniture's small feet.

ON-GRADE

An on-grade patio is the simplest type of patio to build.
Strictly speaking, all the edges of an on-grade patio are
flush with the surrounding ground. This smooth transition
to the lawn makes on-grade patios appear and "live" bigger,
so they are particularly appropriate when space is limited.
Without drop-offs or level changes they are safe for children's
play areas. On-grade patios obviously require level ground,
but, by altering the grade, it may be possible to construct an
on-grade patio even if your land slopes.

For practical considerations such as rain and snow, an
on-grade patio should be at least 6 in. below the first floor
of a house. Typically, however, the ground is 12 in. or more
below the first floor, which means that a set of steps has to be
used to connect the house with the patio.

▼ SET A STEP OR TWO below a small
bungalow, this on-grade patio takes
advantage of the level site. Beginning
next to the house, the patio flows
between the plantings, right up to the
edge of the pool. The irregular flagstones are in keeping with the casual
nature of the landscaping.

SUNKEN

A sunken patio has one or more sides below the surrounding grade level and typically includes a retaining wall constructed on the sloping ground to hold back the earth. Sunken patios are often combined with on-grade patios and steps to create a two-tiered effect.

In addition to making it possible to build on slopes, sunken patios create a sense of privacy and shelter, providing protection in windy locations. With a southern orientation, they capture and focus the warming sun, which makes them particularly pleasant places in late spring and early fall. And the retaining wall can provide seating or planting opportunities, whether for additional privacy or ambience.

▲ SOMETIMES MOVING JUST A LITTLE DIRT pays big dividends. This low retaining wall was used to widen the path and create a small patio, forming a place for visitors to sit while wandering through the landscape.

▼ RETAINING WALLS CREATE much-needed space around this pool-side patio. The curved wall in the foreground carves out a generous seating area, which feels protected and out of the way, while the stone surfaces offer nice contrast to the concrete pool surround.

RAISED

Raised patios are constructed above the existing ground and are level with, or one step down from, the first floor living spaces. These types of patios include a wall built under the perimeter of the patio. It's more common in these situations for a deck to be used instead of a raised patio (decks cost less), but like any other type of patio, raised versions look and feel more substantial, like the floors of indoor spaces.

▼ ALTHOUGH THE FIRST FLOOR of this home is not too far above grade, the owners wanted a more direct connection with the ground. The solution was to build the first step, which is level with the floor, deep enough to form a patio. A low retaining wall flanks one side, while a second step offers informal seating and wraps around the entire patio.

TYPES OF PATIOS

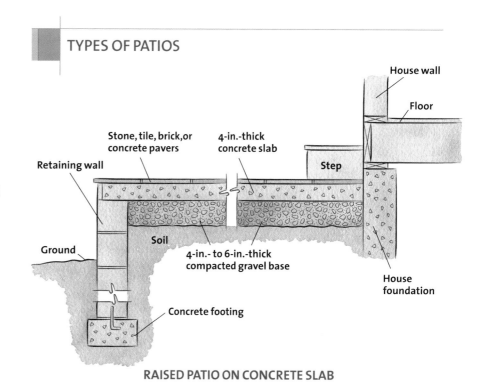

RAISED PATIO ON CONCRETE SLAB

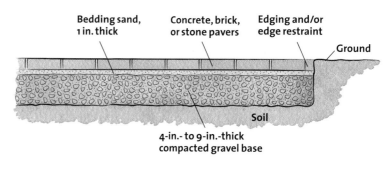

ON-GRADE PATIO ON A GRAVEL BASE

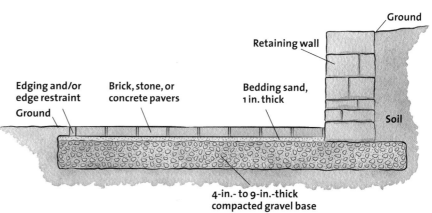

SUNKEN PATIO ON A GRAVEL BASE

► THIS SMALL CORNER PATIO was constructed from ordinary concrete block. This material should only be used temporarily because it's not formulated to withstand the rigors of outdoor exposure and will deteriorate over a relatively short period of time.

▼ THE PLANTING BEDS THAT BORDER this raised patio not only form a clear boundary, but they also camouflage the transition down to the surrounding landscape. The mortar joints, which are flush with the top of the brick pavers, create a fairly even surface for the narrow feet of the chairs.

▲ SMALL URBAN LOTS REQUIRE creative patio solutions. Connected to the front door and the walkway to the curb, this patio provides a transition place for guests coming and going.

▲ THIS BI-LEVEL PATIO has an upper seating area and a lower dining space. The retaining wall of the sunken portion wraps around the outside chimney and adds a separate seating area.

◄ IN ANTIQUE PARLANCE, a married piece is something that is constructed from two or more parts that didn't originally go together. This table—with its barrel bottom and stone top—is a good example of a married piece that works and complements the many textures of the stone sitting area and surrounding plantings.

Walkways to and from the Home

ON THE MOST BASIC LEVEL, WALKWAYS are routes of travel used to get from point A to point B. Around the home they lead guests to the front door, connect the back door to a secluded patio or pool, or meander through a flower garden. But they can do much more than that. Carefully planned, walkways and paths create an organizational structure, efficiently linking the different parts of your landscape in a way that's aesthetically pleasing. This network of walkways can be broken down into a hierarchy of three categories, based primarily on how they're used and their relative size.

▲ THE SHARP CONTRAST between the red tile pavers and landscape helps to clearly define this walkway. The view of the fireplace pulls you forward, but the mid-walkway planting encourages you to slow down and enjoy the surroundings.

◄ THE IMPORTANCE OF THIS SIDE ENTRANCE is noted by the two primary walkways that lead to the porch and door. A secondary, stepping-stone walkway branches off to the left, giving the impression that visitors come to the front door much less frequently.

PRIMARY WALKWAYS

Primary walkways are the widest type of walkway, generously accommodating two people walking side by side, and are usually the most frequently traveled. They may stand alone or have other walks branching off of them. A walk to a front door is an obvious example, but a wide walk from the garage to the house or one that leads from a patio through the lawn also can be considered a primary walkway.

The material chosen for a primary walkway is important, since the walk not only needs to look good but also has to provide safe footing. Loose materials that are likely to get tracked into the house and are difficult to clear of snow are not the best choices for front-door walks.

▶ THIS PATH IS INTENTIONALLY NARROW and was constructed with material that requires a slow pace, so that the lush plantings can be enjoyed. The curving line is not only beautiful, but also adds a sense of mystery to the experience.

Calling All Professionals

THE RIGHT PROS CAN OFFER SAGE ADVICE and produce higher quality results than most do-it-yourselfers. Here's a short list of some of the professionals you might consider hiring.

■ A **LANDSCAPE ARCHITECT** is a design professional that has graduated from an accredited landscape architecture school, passed an exam, and is licensed by the American Society of Landscape Architects®. These pros are trained in all aspects of landscape design including space planning, land forms, and plant selection. Landscape architects often act as construction managers for larger landscape projects, overseeing the work and verifying that it is built according to the specifications.

Landscape designers, on the other hand, may have some professional training and provide services similar to a landscape architect's, but landscape designers are not licensed.

■ A **LANDSCAPING CONTRACTOR** actually builds a landscape project. A large contractor might employ all the people—such as heavy equipment operators, masons, gardeners, and laborers—required to complete even the biggest job. Small firms may do only a portion of the job themselves and subcontract the rest.

■ AN **EXCAVATING CONTRACTOR** operates heavy equipment, such as backhoes and bulldozers, and is often needed during the construction phase to dig trenches, excavate holes, or reshape the ground.

■ A **MASON** is a skilled worker who builds walls, patios, and steps with brick, stone, tile, or concrete. Some masons specialize in certain types of projects or materials. If you hire a mason, be sure his or her skills are compatible with your project.

SECONDARY WALKWAYS

Secondary walkways may branch off of primary walkways or stand alone. Although they are narrower than primary walkways, secondary walkways often provide adequate space for people to walk side by side. Sometimes they're utilitarian in nature and should be wide enough to accommodate a person pushing a wheelbarrow or carrying a trash can. As with primary walkways, the materials for secondary paths should be compatible with how they're used.

▶ SEEMINGLY STITCHED TOGETHER at irregular intervals with grass seams, this informal, secondary walkway wanders through an iron gate. The adjacent plantings alter the walk's width and provide contrast against the gray, washed stones.

▼ THIS PRIMARY WALKWAY leading to the front door is intersected by a secondary garden walk of loose fill material. Their different widths and contrasting materials make a clear distinction between them.

TERTIARY WALKWAYS

A thin necklace of stepping stones or a delicate ribbon of pea stone, tertiary walkways are the narrowest of all walkways. Perhaps best described as paths, they are traveled single file and sometimes require that, to stay on track, travelers pay close attention to where they step. Tertiary walkways are perfect for accessing out-of-the-way patios or secret gardens, especially when the paths are bordered by lush plantings.

▲ TWO STEPS AND A LOW retaining wall serve to separate the front lawn from the side yard, while the narrow walkway offers an open invitation to enter this more private area. The curving path signals a more casual tone to this seating area.

◄ THE LATE AFTERNOON SUN beckons as it surrounds this pair of chairs and reflects off the stepping-stone path. To stay on the path requires thoughtful, measured steps, setting the mood for quiet conversation.

BEGINNINGS AND ENDINGS

To create a truly successful walkway there are a couple of other elements, in addition to width, that need to be considered. Every walkway has a beginning—an entrance—and it should be clearly defined. Gates, brick pillars, large rocks, wooden posts, a pergola, or simply a change in the walking surface are effective ways to mark an entrance.

The destination, or goal, is another important aspect of walkway design. Every walkway, whether it leads to the front door or to a quiet bench, has a final destination. However, if a walkway is particularly long, or to create visual interest, you also may want to introduce an intermediate goal—such as a statue, piece of sculpture, or garden ornament—to entice the walker onward.

▲ THIS BRICK WALKWAY IS INLAID with a diagonal design of concrete pavers that emphasizes the transition from one place to another. The pavers also add some punch to this otherwise sedate path.

◄ ▼ CAREFULLY ARRANGED OPEN SIDE DOWN on the pea stones, bleached clamshells adorn the edges of this wide garden path. Plants positioned at regular intervals along the straight path will, over time, transform the direct line of travel into a more leisurely one.

▲ ALTHOUGH THE END IS NOWHERE IN SIGHT, the slow-moving stream and lyrical waterfall make traveling this path more about the journey than the destination. The path widens at the falls to create a place to stop and contemplate the surroundings.

◄ PEACEFULLY HUNG IN A GLADE of tall trees adjacent to a footbridge, this hammock is accessed by some steps that actually look more like a stepping-stone path.

Tying Places Together with Steps

I T IS THE RARE HOUSE THAT IS BUILT on a perfectly level piece of ground. Whether the land is gently sloping or steeply pitched, stairs are needed to negotiate changes in elevation. In addition to their functional aspects, steps can be used as design elements to make a bold statement, or they can integrate seamlessly into the landscape. Steps often are constructed at the beginning, middle, or end of walkways, and are built to match their width. On-grade steps can be categorized by the materials and methods used to build them.

▼ THE RECTANGULAR SHAPE of the bricks that compose these mortared steps complements the formal plantings that border the swimming pool. To ensure safety and comfort, outdoor steps typically have a lower rise than those inside the house.

MORTARED STEPS

Typically built with brick, concrete pavers, or stone, the treads and risers of mortared steps are held together with cement. This gives them a rigid structure and formal look that is most appropriate for a primary walkway to the front door. In parts of the country where the ground freezes, frost will likely break the mortar, requiring repairs that may be costly and difficult.

▶ WIDE, LOW, AND SLEEK, this flight of steps is perfectly scaled for a grand entrance. The wall, risers, and foundation veneer all are made from the same stone, which unifies and completes the composition.

Understanding Stairs

I F YOU'RE CONSIDERING making a flight of on-grade stairs part of your landscape, you'll want to be familiar with the four basic concepts of stair design and construction—rise, run, riser, and tread. The first two, rise and run, are units of measure, while riser and tread are stair components.

- **RISE** is a vertical distance. The unit of rise, 6 in., for example, is the height of an individual step, while the total rise is the distance from the bottom of the steps to the top.

- **RUN** is a measure of horizontal distance, or length. The unit of run, 16 in., for example, is the depth of one step, and the total run is the overall length of the entire set of steps, from the first riser to the last.

- **A RISER** is a physical object that spans the unit of rise. An on-grade riser is typically a solid piece of wood, a timber, for example, or a stone or stones.

- **TREADS** span individual units of run and are often stone, brick, or concrete, but also can be the earth itself, sometimes topped with another material.

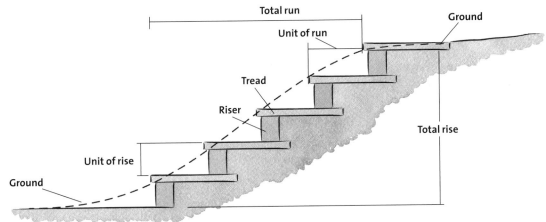

DRY-LAID STEPS

Dry-laid steps are constructed without mortar and instead are held together by their weight and gravity. They use multiple-piece risers and single- or multiple-piece treads made of stone or of precast concrete pieces similar to concrete pavers. While dry-laid steps, like mortared steps, should be constructed on an appropriate base, they can flex with changes caused by freezing and thawing.

▼ ALTHOUGH THEY ARE PHYSICALLY LARGE, these gray steps actually play second fiddle to the colorful retaining walls and strong visual pattern of the patio. The top step is a perfect place to sit down, lean up against the wall, and take in the view.

STEPS WITH INFILL TREADS

When steps are carved into a hillside, retaining walls are sometimes needed to hold back the earth along the sides of the stair. Steps with infill treads eliminate that need. Typically constructed with wood or composite landscaping timbers, the risers and sides of the steps form a box. The box is filled with a free-draining material, such as crushed gravel, and then the finish tread material is added on top. The finish treads can be virtually any material—washed stone, wood chips, stone, brick or concrete pavers, or even grass.

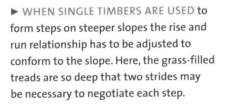

▶ WHEN SINGLE TIMBERS ARE USED to form steps on steeper slopes the rise and run relationship has to be adjusted to conform to the slope. Here, the grass-filled treads are so deep that two strides may be necessary to negotiate each step.

◀ CONTRAST AND CRISPNESS are the bywords for this raised patio and steps. The red of the stuccoed retaining wall matches the tile risers. A thin edge of white marble draws a sharp distinction between the vertical and horizontal surfaces.

ONE-PIECE STEPS

One-piece steps are typically built with large stones, each one large enough to form both the riser and tread. This means that the stones need to be between 4 in. and 6 in. thick and 14 in. to 20 in. deep. These types of steps are natural-looking and blend into the landscape nicely.

▶ ON A GENTLE SLOPE, a set of steps can easily be made by digging the bottom of landscaping timbers into the ground and fastening them securely. The top of the timbers—set flush with the ground—form the tread.

▼ BOULDERS SAVED DURING EXCAVATION mark this long flight of steps, which is broken up with landings at regular intervals. Landings not only allow the total run and rise of the steps to be adjusted to match the height of the hill, but they also let people pause to catch their breath as they make their way up the long ascent.

RISER-ONLY STEPS

Perhaps the simplest steps are riser-only steps—they are built to follow the slope of a hill and generally are built directly on the existing ground, without a prepared base. Landscaping timbers (both wood and composite), thick planks, and even small-diameter logs are used for the risers, while grass, wood chips, or mulch form the treads.

▲ SIMPLICITY CAN BE STRIKING. This semicircular dry-laid step, constructed to match the span of the porch posts and topped with a single stone, was designed to be a focal point at the home's entrance.

▼ AT FIRST GLANCE the brick nosing on this low step appears to be merely a design statement (tying the step to the adjacent wall), but the nosing also serves a practical purpose. The change in material helps distinguish the change in elevation, making the step easier to see and safer to navigate.

Walls in the Landscape

▲ THIS LONG RETAINING WALL, constructed with large fieldstones, and the adjacent stepping-stone path blend perfectly with the surroundings and the shingled house to which they lead.

WALLS HAVE BEEN A PART of our environment since humans first began to build. Perhaps it's that long history that makes them seem right at home in the landscape. Walls are used to sculpt the earth and mark boundaries, but they create visual beauty too, merging with the natural surroundings or adding a decorative element.

There are two general types of walls—freestanding and retaining. While both types can be built with a number of different materials, there are two basic construction methods—dry-laid and mortared. Dry-laid walls rely on their own weight, on friction, and on proper design and construction techniques to hold together. This somewhat limits the materials that can be used to construct them. Mortared walls are bound together by cement mortar—a mixture of portland cement, sand, lime, and water. The mortared joints permit the use of rounded stones and bricks. Although both dry-laid and mortared walls need to be constructed on a stable base, the latter should be supported by a steel-reinforced concrete footing to avoid cracking.

▼ A FREESTANDING WALL ANCHORS THIS CIRCULAR PATIO. The strength of the wall's large, rugged stones holds its own against the power of the bright red pavers, striking an effective balance.

▲ THE MUTED TONES AND SIMPLE LINES of this retaining wall and walkway make the house stand out as the focal point of the entry. Simple plantings reinforce the effect.

FREESTANDING WALLS

Freestanding walls rest on top of the ground and have two finished faces. They are used to separate different landscape areas from each other and to add visual interest. Elements such as seats and planters often are incorporated into freestanding walls; when built about 18 in. high, the whole wall becomes a bench. Tall freestanding walls create privacy and can turn an outdoor space into an outdoor room.

▲ LEADING FROM A GENEROUS SET OF STEPS, this sturdy retaining wall seemingly stretches out as far as the eye can see. The wall eliminates an awkward slope, creates two level lawns, and marks a transition point in the landscape.

▼ THIS SMALL FIELDSTONE RETAINING WALL makes room for a set of entry steps. The plantings around the wall mimic the shape of the fieldstones, while the sleek, cut-stone stair treads add a pleasant contrast.

RETAINING WALLS

Retaining walls hold back earth and transform sloping ground into level areas for patios, gardens, and planting beds. On steep sites multiple retaining walls can be used to form a series of terraces that create a gradual transition from the top to the bottom. Depending on the soil conditions and type of material, retaining walls that are taller than 3 ft. may need to be engineered to ensure their stability.

▶ THE STRIKING WHITE STONES used to construct the patio, steps, and retaining walls provide an excellent backdrop for plants, which fill the terraced beds and line the base of the lowest wall. As an extra touch, a small pond backs against the same wall.

▼ PROVING THAT EVEN RECTANGULAR, rigid materials such as bricks or concrete pavers can be fluid, this low wall follows the flow of the path. The broad brick cap protects the wall from the elements and, at about 18 in. high, makes a great place to sit and smell the flowers.

Materials for Patios and Walkways

ASUCCESSFUL PROJECT DEPENDS on three things: good design, quality construction, and proper building materials. Choosing the right materials is key. While you want to choose materials that are attractive, there's more to the decision than meets the eye. Some other factors also should be considered.

Materials should be appropriate for their use—both aesthetically and functionally. For example, if you want to create a formal walkway to your front door, washed stones or wood chips are probably not going to create the right look. Also, these materials can get stuck in shoes and be tracked into your house, which makes them doubly inappropriate.

Patios and walkways are expensive, but don't skimp when buying building materials. They need to stand up to the elements, so choose high-quality, durable types. Some materials age gracefully and develop a pleasing patina over time, while others simply deteriorate.

While it's not possible to build a totally maintenance-free patio or walkway, a little planning and attention to detail can reduce the amount of time devoted to upkeep. For example, walkways that are designed so that a mower can cut right up to and over them will eliminate the need for extensive trimming. And although durable materials and the method of construction will reduce the need for repairs and maintenance, it's always a good idea to consult with construction professionals to determine what's best for your situation and part of the country.

► CONTAINED WITHIN A SIMPLE picket fence, the quiet atmosphere of this small patio is enhanced by the square, basket-weave pattern of the brick pavers. The various colors of these recycled bricks are installed in a random mix, supporting the feel of the space.

▲ THIS PATTERN OF LARGE, square, concrete pavers separated by wide, grass-filled joints makes a bold statement that stands up to the heavy, wooden furniture.

▶ COMBINING DISSIMILAR MATERIALS can take some courage, but the results are often worth the risk. Instead of using a standard border for their concrete paver walkway, the owners went with one of rough stones. The effect is a layered look between walkway, border, and plantings.

Green Building Guidelines

To LESSEN THE IMPACT your patios and walkways will have on the planet you can incorporate earth-friendly practices into your project. Here are some guidelines to help you choose among the various green building options.

Tap Sustainable Resources

- Salvaged products: recycled brick, timbers
- Materials with recycled content: composite materials, glass, rubber
- Locally available/native materials: stone, wood, chips, pine needles
- By-products of other industries: crushed shells (oysters or clams), bark mulch, wood chips
- Products from sustainably managed forests

Choose the Less-Toxic Option

- Alternatives to high VOC-content finishes: latex-based stains and sealers
- Alternatives to wood treated with conventional preservatives: Avoid pentachlorophenol (penta) and creosote. Use naturally insect- and rot-resistant woods, or those treated with alkaline, copper-based preservatives.

Consider Your Impact

- Use eco-friendly construction techniques: Avoid monolith construction. Provide gaps between patio and walkway materials.
- Design to minimize use of motorized maintenance equipment (weed eaters, leaf blowers, mowers): Use low-profile edgings and stepping stones.
- Reduce resource consumption: Use long-lasting materials, such as stone, rot-resistant woods, and rust-resistant fasteners.
- Plan for reduced water use: Plant indigenous species that require less water, and design the landscape to hold water.

► SHAPE IS THE DOMINANT theme here as the prominent curve of this freestanding wall creates a sense of place for the lounge chairs. Although the wall and patio have the same coloration, the slight tension between the dry-laid cut stone of the wall and the patio's irregular flagstones prevents the composition from being bland.

◄ TUCKED BETWEEN the side wall of the house and the rough stone retaining wall, this patio's sinuous line and circular pattern help define the different seating areas. The bistro table occupies the center while the conversation group and chaise lounge seek the edges.

▼ BRIGHTLY COLORED TULIPS appear to light the way to the house, while the large stepping stones provide ample width for two visitors to walk side by side. As it nears the house, this walkway makes a bend around a planting bed, which gives purpose to the curve so that it doesn't feel arbitrary.

▼ CAST-IN-PLACE CONCRETE begins as a liquid material, so it can easily be formed to take many shapes, as evidenced by the sweeping curve of this concrete walkway. Concrete must be installed with joints at regular intervals; bricks are used here, instead of the standard single trowel line.

Patios for Dining and Cooking

PATIOS DESIGNED FOR COOKING AND DINING usually top the list for any new outdoor living space. Perhaps it's the pull of the sun and fresh air, or maybe we have our prehistoric ancestors to thank, but whatever the reason, there's nothing we seem to like more than eating and cooking outdoors. Sure it's romantic, but there are some practical aspects as well. Certain kinds of cooking—such as grilling and smoking—are best done outdoors, and cleaning up is less of a concern.

To ensure that your dining or cooking patio is a success and is used on a regular basis, it should be readily accessible from the indoor kitchen. A location at the end of the house that contains the kitchen is ideal. If there isn't already a door creating a direct path from the indoor kitchen or dining room to the patio, consider installing a wide one. French doors are perfect. Patios that are intended to be used primarily by the family should be positioned as close as possible to the house, while those designed for larger gatherings or entertaining can be farther away; walkways or a series of smaller patios can help maintain a connection to the house.

◄ THIS DINING PATIO is large enough to be functional, yet small enough to feel intimate. Dense plantings add color and fragrance and, most important, hide the spot from surrrounding buildings.

Family Dining

▲ STRONG GEOMETRIC SHAPES lend an air of formality to this raised, tile dining patio. With the grilling equipment set up in one corner (not shown), the focus is on dining rather than cooking.

THE FRENZIED PACE AND JAM-PACKED SCHEDULES of everyday life can make family mealtime a rare event. A patio designed for family dining may be just the lure you need to pull everyone together, even if it's just for an hour or so. And there's no question that a patio will spice up the dining experience, even if dinner is only takeout.

Ease of use is important for frequently used family dining patios. It's best to build them so that they're no more than two or three steps below the first floor of the house. This arrangement not only makes the patio feel closer to the house, but also makes serving the meal easier. To avoid tipsy tables and wobbly chairs choose surface materials that are relatively level and bump-free.

Don't skimp on the size of your patio. Measure your existing dining room and table to get a sense of how much space is needed for your family to feel comfortable. But keep in mind that outdoor spaces feel smaller than indoor ones so you'll probably want to increase the size of your patio accordingly. A larger patio also offers more options for table size and position, so that you can accommodate more people as needed, sitting or standing, and adjust for sun and shade as well.

▼ WITH NUMEROUS STYLES of outdoor furniture to choose from you're sure to create just the right atmosphere for any outdoor space. These wicker wing-back chairs encourage family members or guests to relax long after the meal is over. Serving is made easy by the nearby French doors.

▲ A LARGE, SPREADING TREE SHADES THE CORNER of this on-grade patio, making it a perfect spot for a relaxing meal. The pavers, installed in a simple basket-weave pattern, and the high-backed benches turn what might have been a formal space into a family-friendly atmosphere.

◄ TABLES WITH PEDESTAL BASES, such as this glass-top version, allow legs to fit comfortably underneath and make it easy to add more chairs for unexpected friends.

► THIS LONG PATIO was specifically designed to create two different dining areas. In the corner, totally covered by the porch roof, is a small and intimate spot. The other dining area pushes out into the sun and is sized for larger gatherings.

◄ THE ABUNDANCE of flowering plants climbing the garden walls provides fragrance as well as privacy. The setting, even though relatively close to the house, encourages relaxation and lingering.

Types of Furniture

- **WOOD:** can be heavy, depending on the type of construction; requires regular maintenance in the form of paint, stain, or sealer; may or may not be rot resistant, depending on species; vulnerable to rot at joints and at bottoms of the leg

- **NATURAL WICKER:** relatively lightweight; made from natural fibers, such as rattan; usually requires cushions to be comfortable; most natural wicker is not rated for use in uncovered areas; painted wicker has to be repainted from time to time

- **SYNTHETIC WICKER:** relatively lightweight; since it's made from materials such as vinyl resins or fiberglass, it may have an unnatural shine; rated for outdoor use, no maintenance is required

- **PLASTIC:** very lightweight; made from molded plastic resins; rated for outdoor use; may degrade in the sun; no maintenance is required

- **WROUGHT OR CAST IRON:** very heavy; rated for outdoor use but will rust unless painted regularly

- **PAINTED STEEL:** relatively lightweight; rated for outdoor use; paint will crack and peel over time and frames will rust; can be sanded and repainted

- **POWDER-COATED ALUMINUM:** very lightweight, so may be blown by high winds; aluminum tubes are covered with polyester powders baked onto the surface; fabric seats and backs are very durable; no maintenance is required; if coating wears away aluminum will not rust

▲ FLEXIBILITY IS KEY for family dining areas. The two groupings of chairs away from the table offer a place to break away from dining activity. In a pinch, the same chairs can quickly be recruited for a meal.

▼ THE FORMALITY of the neatly trimmed hedges and square flagstones provides the perfect backdrop for the simple, sturdy lines of this wooden dining furniture. Benches are great seats for squirming children and also allow more people to squeeze along the side of a table than chairs do.

◄ ▼ WHILE PRIVACY was of the utmost concern when planning this intimate dining patio, care was taken not to create a claustrophobic cubicle. The square lattice walls, in combination with the climbing vine, screen most of the view from outside; privacy will increase over time, as the vine grows and fills out. The low brick wall serves a dual purpose—it provides a solid visual base for the lightweight lattice and doubles as a planter.

▲ ANCHORED BY AN IMPRESSIVE raised-hearth fireplace and enclosed by a long counter and tall fence, this large dining patio allows kids to run around and adults to mingle within the same area.

► THE RUSTIC SHINGLE SIDING, rough flagstone patio, and bright yellow furniture set the stage for laid-back country dining. Although chairs with arms take up more space at the table than armless types, they are more comfortable and encourage people to settle in and relax.

◄ URBAN NEIGHBORHOODS
typically have small lots and a healthy
dose of noise. This patio area makes the
most of the space, with a tall fence for
privacy and an enclosed water feature
for serenity.

▲ NESTLED BY A CORNER OF THE
HOUSE, this simple patio is only a few
inches lower than the floor inside,
which makes it easy to go in and out.
The long, rectangular, multi-colored
flagstones visually enlarge the space.

◄ THE CHECKERBOARD edg-
ing around this patio signals the
homeowner's desire to blend it into
the landscape. It looks like the grass
is slowly encroaching on the patio,
making it appear that the patio has
been there for years.

Dining under Cover

AS ENJOYABLE AS IT IS TO EAT OUTDOORS, the experience can be enhanced by adding an overhead structure—such as an umbrella, awning, or pergola—to your patio. Adding some sort of cover overhead has a number of benefits, the most important of which is that it helps create a comfortable atmosphere. Sheltered, people can relax and interact without the glare of the sun in their eyes, or its heat beating down on their shoulders.

Today, umbrellas and awnings come in different shapes and sizes, and many also are waterproof; the supple fabric coverings can add a colorful design element as well. Many of them also have options that allow for quick repositioning to keep guests comfortable, whether from sun or rain.

Pergolas also provide relief from the sun, though the roof members have to be closely spaced to provide adequate shade. Climbing vines can be trained to grow over the pergola as well, creating the ultimate natural covering.

▲ SET AGAINST THE OUTDOORS these massive posts connote strength without being overwhelming, thanks to the colorful and lush plantings that help them blend in. The low roof also helps bring a sense of intimacy to the area.

▼ THIS PERGOLA, with its large posts and roof components, has a strong visual impact and is a good example of how an overhead structure can help turn a plain outdoor space into a stylish outdoor room.

▲ THE SIMPLE, BLACK STEEL FRAME of this pergola complements the refined stone and helps visually separate the fireplace and dining area from the pool area. A frosted Plexiglas® roof diffuses the sunlight—and keeps diners dry when showers move in.

◄ THIS WHITE PERGOLA FEELS LIKE an extension of the house because it's the same color as the house trim. The bistro table is just the right size for the modest dining patio, and the plants climbing up the sides of the pergola provide intimacy.

▶ THE DEEP, WEATHERPROOF roof that shelters a large portion of this patio makes it possible to use upholstered chairs. The post, roof structure, and mantle are painted the same color to blend in with the stone fireplace.

▲ PAINTING THE CEILING of the overhead structure white bounces the light deep into this dining patio, preventing it from being too dark. Over time, the climbing ivy will cover the bare concrete-block wall with a lush, green veneer.

▶ IN ADDITION TO AESTHETICS, overhead structures also can serve practical functions. Elegantly curved, the wide ribs of this arbor shade the dining table below from direct exposure to the sun.

► THIS PERGOLA'S WOODEN ROOF members are spaced relatively close together. In the early morning or late in the afternoon, when the sun is low in the sky, they block its rays, creating a blanket of shade.

An Array of Awnings

I F YOU LIVE IN A PART OF THE COUNTRY where hot, sunny days are the norm, or if your patio has a southern or western exposure and sometimes gets unbearably warm, consider installing an awning. There are several different types, and the fabric coverings are available in myriad colors and styles. In addition to shading your patio, awnings can shade large windows, preventing the rooms inside from overheating.

Fixed Awnings

- Are affixed to a building and/or supported by poles and framework
- Cover more area than retractable awnings
- Typically have a more finished, architectural look than retractable types
- Might reduce usable space or disrupt views, due to support pole placement

Retractable Awnings

- Can be adjusted according to the sun's location to provide shade
- Can be motorized to provide easy operation
- Can include a sensor to trigger operation based on wind velocity or degree of sunlight
- Do not require support poles
- Cover less area than other types of awnings

Canopy Awnings

- Have a pitched shape similar to the roof of a house
- Shed water to the sides of patios
- Can be fixed or retractable

Outrigger Awnings

- Combine advantages of fixed and retractable awnings
- Use poles to provide deeper coverage but also feature retractable awnings
- Use poles to provide extra stability for retractable awning
- Use poles that can easily be removed and stored

▲ THIS GENEROUSLY SIZED PERGOLA has virtually turned this patio into a detached suite of outdoor rooms: a dining room, living room, and, adjacent to the large fireplace, a kitchen.

◄ ALTHOUGH THE THIN ROOF CABLES don't create much shade, it's only a matter of time before the well-established grapevines spread to form a bright green, summer umbrella of leaves. Of course, they'll disappear in the fall, allowing the sun to warm the dining area during autumn and spring.

Outdoor Kitchens

I F YOU LOVE TO COOK FOR FRIENDS AND FAMILY and enjoy being out-doors, you may want to indulge both passions by building an outdoor kitchen. A significant step up from the portable grill, outdoor kitchens typically are comprised of permanent counters and built-in equipment. Self-contained, outdoor kitchens are less dependent on support from their indoor relatives, and can be built away from the house. Often, they are built in conjunction with a larger outdoor dining space, creating a destination.

The issues confronted when planning an outdoor kitchen are, for the most part, similar to those for the indoor variety—the work triangle, counter space, storage space—with one major exception: the weather. And nothing influences the weather quite like geography. If you're in a part of the coun-try where outdoor living is possible during a significant portion of the year, investing in a full-blown outdoor kitchen probably makes more sense than if you experience only two seasons—winter and the fourth of July.

▶ LOCATED OFF TO ONE SIDE of the patio, this outdoor kitchen exempli-fies careful planning and attention to detail. An efficient L-shaped counter places the sink closer to the seating group, while the potentially smoke-producing gas grill is farther away. The fire pit ties the whole space together, since it's effectively in the center of dining, relaxing, and cooking activities.

▶ ALTHOUGH IT'S ABOUT THE SAME SIZE as a portable unit, this grill looks substantial and has a sense of perma-nence because it's built into the stone wall. The double doors enclose plenty of easy-to-access storage and the top of the wall creates much-needed counter space.

◄ ► HERE'S AN EXAMPLE of how a sleek modern material, stainless steel, can be beautifully combined with a building material that's centuries old. The stone wall has the physical presence to carry the visual weight of the oversized grill, and the meticulous installation of the stonework complements the precise nature of the steel.

◄ ► ONE OF THE PLAYFUL circular patterns used in this expansive patio defines the grilling station. A distinctive border of red concrete pavers emphasizes the step down to the adjacent sitting area; the step might otherwise be hard to see.

◄ THE CHEFS WHO GRILL UP meals served on this dining patio are rewarded for all their hard work with a beautiful view of the nearby lake. The irregular flagstones and the wall built with native fieldstone harmonize with the rural environment.

► TAKING ITS CUE from indoor kitchens, the same thick stone countertop material is used for the backsplash, forming a narrow ledge that's handy for holding small items, such as cooking spices.

Outdoor Kitchen Equipment Choices

MOST FULL-SERVICE OUTDOOR KITCHENS enable the chef to prepare the entire meal in the open air. But that requires a full complement of equipment. Some of the items you may want in your outdoor kitchen include:

- Grill—gas, charcoal, or both
- Separate cooktop
- Warming oven
- Deep-fat fryer
- Smoker
- Refrigerator
- Sink
- Dishwasher

Of course, this equipment requires utility hookups, such as electricity, water, and fuel (propane or natural gas). Remember that the cost of installing utilities goes up as the distance between the outdoor kitchen and house increases.

▲ BUILT-IN STAINLESS STEEL GRILL

► UNDER-COUNTER REFRIGERATOR

Outdoor Entertaining

EVEN THE SMALLEST OF YARDS can incorporate a patio designed for entertaining. While some will allow for multiple seating areas and an outdoor fireplace, others might only have space for a couple of chairs around a small table or fire pit. So as you plan this type of space, first consider your lifestyle and the kind of gatherings you're likely to have. Rectilinear layouts and refined materials establish a formal atmosphere, while designs that are free flowing and built with rougher materials are more informal in nature.

When designing the layout, shape your patio and arrange your furniture to reflect the way people interact at social gatherings. People tend to gather in small groups, so instead of making one or two large seating arrangements, create several smaller ones for four to six. Some folks like to be right in the middle of the action while others prefer to be literally on the periphery, so be sure to include some seating along an edge of the patio. Of course no seating arrangement is going to be perfect, but if your outdoor furniture is light and easy to move, your guests will rearrange it to suit the moment.

▲ A LARGE SEATING GROUP, centered on this patio, holds court and invites active conversation. The formally styled furniture, as well as the mix of seating arrangements, clearly indicates that this is a place where adults can get away from the house to socialize.

▼ THESE IVY-COVERED WALLS and rich brick pavers make the perfect atmosphere for dining alfresco in the fading light of day. The lightweight bench can easily be pulled up to the table to accommodate more than two guests.

▲ THIS PATIO OFFERS something for everyone. The sun-shy can hang out in the shade of the wooden pergola, while those who prefer warmth can sit at the uncovered counter, or pull a chair up to the fire. The raised hearth offers additional seating.

◄ SPREAD OUT AROUND an open fire, this seating arrangement is perfect for taking in the view and relaxing until well into the night. The wide arms of the Adirondack-style chairs are virtual side tables, with ample space to rest a drink.

◄ SERVED IN THIS out-of-the-way corner, any meal becomes a special occasion. The high, curving wall shelters and defines the space. And although the table setting is quite elaborate, the high-backed wicker chairs have enough presence to tie the whole scene together.

▼ THE WIDE OPEN SPACES of this regular-flagstone patio provide plenty of room for entertaining, but it's the space-enclosing wall that is perhaps most interesting. Built-in planters and jogs that create conversation nooks make the space feel less grand.

Types of Fire Pits

$\mathcal{S}$ITTING AROUND AN OPEN FIRE is an archetypal experience that you can bring to your patio by installing a fire pit. Despite their name, most modern fire pits are placed on top of the ground, although the bottom of some may be installed below grade. There are many options available.

- **RAISED, FREESTANDING FIRE PITS:** Often shaped like bowls or pots, freestanding fire pits are self-contained, supported on legs, and portable. Made from materials such as copper, cast iron, or stainless or porcelain-coated steel, they are fueled with wood or charcoal.

- **BUILT-IN FIRE PITS:** Either raised above or partially buried in the ground, built-in fire pits are, as the name suggests, immovable. They can be constructed with a number of different materials, such as stone, concrete block, or poured concrete, and finished with tile or stucco.

- **FIRE-PIT TABLES:** Usually made of stone or reinforced concrete, fire-pit tables provide a place for eating and have a space in the middle to hold a self-contained fire pit that's typically fired with natural gas or propane.

- **CHIMINEAS:** These are basically small, portable, outdoor fire-places with a fire box and short chimney. They are made from fired clay and cast iron and are typically fueled by wood.

- **PORTABLE FIRE RINGS:** Made from cast iron or steel, fire rings can be disassembled and moved from place to place. Most use wood or charcoal and some come with grids for cooking; they typically do not have bottoms.

A Simple Fire Pit

THIS FIRE PIT IS CONSTRUCTED with concrete pavers and a steel ring, which can be found at many garden and home centers. Dry-laid, wedge-shaped concrete blocks form an inside diameter of approximately 36 in. and an exterior diameter of about 48 in., and create a pit that's four courses high. You can modify the size of the pit to suit your needs by using materials of different sizes.

STEP 1: Clear the ground of grass and sod, then dig a hole about 8 in. deep and a foot larger than the finished pit, in this case 5 ft. in diameter. Fill the hole with about 6 in. of firmly compacted gravel.

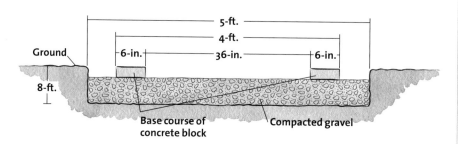

Ground
5-ft.
4-ft.
6-in. 36-in. 6-in.
8-ft.
Base course of concrete block
Compacted gravel

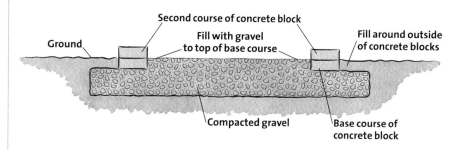

Second course of concrete block
Fill with gravel to top of base course
Fill around outside of concrete blocks
Ground
Compacted gravel
Base course of concrete block

STEP 2: To guide the placement of the base course of concrete block, place the steel ring in the center of the hole. Lay the base course of block around the ring; although the blocks don't have to touch the ring, they should fit under its lip. Make sure each block is level. Backfill the outside of the circle with some of the excavated earth. Then remove the steel ring from the hole and fill it with gravel up to the top of the base course.

STEP 3: Install the next two courses. Be sure to keep them flush with the edges of the lower course, checking your accuracy with the steel ring. When the third course is finished, install the steel ring, then add the final two courses of block.

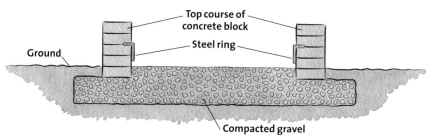

Top course of concrete block
Steel ring
Ground
Compacted gravel

Because this pit is created from dry-laid blocks, some of the blocks may be knocked out of alignment from time to time. If that happens, adjust the misaligned blocks by tapping them with a rubber mallet or heavy piece of wood.

▲ THIS PATIO IS A CAREFUL STUDY in red and green, clean lines, and flat planes. The horizontal composition of the built-in couch, coffee table, and fire pit is set against a thin wall and seems to float above the smooth, concrete patio surface. The table completes the look.

◄ THE RUSTIC NATURE OF THIS SPACE— from the pea-stone patio and the stone table up to the overhanging tree branches—sets the tone for casual dining and conversation.

DINING UNDER LIGHTS

▶ CANDLES AND DINING go hand in hand. An actual candelabrum hangs above the dining table, suspended from the pergola, while multiple candles adorn the fireplace. Using candles for lighting, of course, eliminates the need to run electricity, but be prepared to relight them when the wind blows unless they are enclosed.

▲ WHILE CANDLES CAN CAST just the right amount of light for a romantic dinner, the large picture windows also provide a soft glow of light from inside.

▶ THESE COLORFUL LANTERNS were chosen for the splash of color they add during the day, as well as the light they provide at night. When illuminated, additional lamps on the other side of the patio add an unobtrusive brightness to the seating area.

▲ THIS PAIR OF METAL-SHADE DOWNLIGHTS will provide plenty of illumination. To ensure just the right amount of light, utilize dimmer switches.

Decorating with Nature

► ONE OF THE EASIEST WAYS to redecorate a room is to give it a fresh coat of paint. Although patios aren't surrounded by walls, you can still color the surroundings with flowering plants. Set up a layered effect of pots, placing them at different heights—some on the patio floor, a few on plant stands, and others hung where possible.

▲ RED FLOWERS WELCOME ALL to this delicate-looking gazebo. Using the same flowers and color to adorn the table and window boxes makes the look more dramatic than if multiple species and shades were used.

◄ ► THE BEAUTY OF POTTED PLANTS lies not only in the flowers and foliage, but also in their containers. There's as much of an art to choosing the right pot as there is to picking the proper plant. Available in a wide range of colors, styles, and materials, containers can complement a plant's color and shape, blending into the background, or contrast sharply, demanding attention.

▲ VISIBLE FROM THE NEARBY DINING TABLE, the highlight of this patio and planting bed is the small, natural-looking pond. Its position, nestled against the rock outcropping, makes it stand out against the otherwise green background.

Patios
for Relaxing

PEOPLE OFTEN DREAM OF THE OUTDOORS—the deep woods, an isolated lake, or a deserted stretch of ocean beach—when they want to escape their cares and recharge their psyches. But for most of us, going to one of those destinations requires two weeks of vacation, a tidy sum of money, and a long trip by car or plane. However, you can create a personal retreat right in your own backyard.

Whether used to enjoy an after-breakfast cup of coffee, a quiet conversation with a special friend, a particularly nice view, or some uninterrupted reading or meditation, leisure patios can be a haven. When considering a patio for true relaxation, there are a few things to keep in mind. Because they are typically used by only one or two people, these patios are often intimate in size. And, unlike patios that encourage activity and lively discussions, leisure patios should be designed to calm the senses. With that in mind, any space in your landscape can likely qualify, whether it's directly off the house or in the farthest corner of your yard.

◄ THE CANOPY FORMED BY TREE BRANCHES allows only dappled sunlight, keeping this patio cool during summer's heat. Deep steps leading to the patio require a slower pace, helping guests shift into relaxation mode.

Patios Connected to the House

I
T MIGHT SEEM LIKE A TOUGH CHALLENGE to construct a patio that provides the kind of tranquil atmosphere you desire adjacent to your house, but careful planning can ensure success. First, determine where along the house to position your patio by answering a few questions: How do you intend to use your patio—as a place to socialize with a friend or two, or as a private spot all to yourself? (Either way, you may have to screen the patio from the neighbors.) What time of the day are you most likely to use your patio—in the morning, around noon, or in the evening? How much space do you need? Do you find very small spaces cozy or claustrophobic?

An important part of relaxing on a patio is comfortable furniture. Not only should it feel good, but it also should complement the way you like to relax. Is your idea of total bliss stretching out on a chaise lounge, or would you prefer to swing gently back and forth in a gliding chair? Do you want a place to set down a drink or book? There's no reason you can't make your outdoor "away" spot every bit as inviting as one indoors.

▲ THE TALL PLANTINGS AND LOW PALM TREE create an alcove-like space, screened from the house. Although the metal furniture harmonizes with the natural surroundings, the chairs aren't intended for long hours of laid-back conversation.

◄ LOCATED IN A QUIET CORNER, partially sheltered by the overhead awning and arranged in a conversation-encouraging semicircle, these wicker chairs invite you to kick off your shoes and stay awhile.

◀ ▲ WITH THE EXCEPTION OF ONE OPEN SECTION, the tall latticework fence completely encloses this personal retreat. From a distance, the small diagonal openings within the lattice make it difficult to see in, and soften the light that flows into the space. Although the opening might compromise privacy, the bistro table is pulled over to the side, hiding it from the most public views.

◄ FILTERED SUNLIGHT WARMS this comfortable seating group, which is located away from the entry door and out of the dark end of the patio. The latticework screen at the far end blocks the neighbors' view, enhancing privacy created by the walls of the house.

▲ TUCKED OUT OF THE WAY off the main patio, this quiet spot is enhanced by the simplicity of the setup. Without the sunny yellow umbrella, this area might be a bit bland.

◄ THE VIBRANT COLORS in this setting don't make it any less relaxing, thanks to the built-in bench with cushions and pillows. While waterproof cushions are available, unattached versions like these are easy to bring inside to keep dry from rain or dew.

◄ WHILE THESE ADIRONDACK-STYLE CHAIRS are clearly positioned to soak up the sun, they can easily be moved under the shade of the pergola. Chairs like these, with wide arms, high backs, and footrests, naturally encourage you to linger.

▼ A GURGLING FOUNTAIN helps to mark the entrance to this informal, conversation patio. With the chairs backed by the wall and flanked by high-growing plantings, this seating group feels surprisingly protected.

◄ THERE'S NOTHING QUITE AS SOOTHING as the back and forth motion of a swing—it's the epitome of relaxation. While they can be incorporated into most any type of setting, every swing needs structural supports designed to withstand the forces the swing's motion exerts.

▼ LOCATED DIRECTLY OFF a large living space, this patio invites two or three people to break away from perhaps a bigger group for a more private conversation. Although the seating group is exposed to the house, it's positioned out of the line of travel, and the tall hedge screens it from more public spaces in the yard.

Positioning a Patio for Privacy

Y OU'LL ENJOY YOUR PATIO much more and find it more relaxing if it's positioned to avoid intrusions, whether from people, pets, or noise.

- To ensure that the least amount of traffic crosses the patio, position it to one side or the other of any doors that lead out of the house.

- To create more privacy, slip the patio around a corner, or screen the side nearest the door.

- To totally separate your patio from active spaces, locate it directly off the master bedroom or private study.

- If a patio is located outside a window, consider installing an external shutter that you can close when you're using the patio.

- To block your view of the neighbors, consider building a solid fence along one or more sides of your patio.

- To muffle extraneous noise, install a fountain or artificial waterfall.

- To enjoy your favorite music, install outdoor speakers.

▲ WITH THE SCENT of fragrant climbing roses, lilies, and other plants all around, this getaway was designed to be a private dining spot. The tall wooden portal creates a subtle sense of entering into a special place.

Screening a Patio from Neighbors

To CREATE PRIVACY, it might be necessary to screen your patio from adjacent streets or neighboring buildings. The quickest, most effective screening method is to build a fence or wall. While the type and style you choose is certainly influenced by your budget, the most important factor is the amount of privacy you desire. If you want to completely block lines of sight into your patio, build a solid fence or wall.

If you are in no rush for privacy, or if you'd like a more natural type of screen, consider planting a hedge. If you want to screen out neighboring second floor windows, plant a tightly spaced row of trees. Fast-growing trees such as Siberian elm or Canadian hemlock can be pruned to form hedges and other species, such as some types of arborvitae and cedar, grow to 30 ft. or more.

If neither of these approaches will work in your situation, a large awning or canopy might be the answer. In addition to overhead screening, fabric sidewalls can be added to block your neighbors' views.

▲ THIS WOODEN STOCKADE FENCE is tall enough to block the view from the neighboring house, while the profusion of flowering plants adds color and texture to what might otherwise have been a drab environment.

▲ SOLID WALLS, such as this one made of stucco, block unwanted noise as well as intrusive sight lines. To avoid a monolithic feeling, the wall rises like a line of rolling hills as it encircles the patio. Rough stone walls form planters that break up the vertical plane of the wall and contrast with its smooth surface.

▲ FENCES HELP CREATE MICROCLIMATES, blocking wind and, when positioned to the north side of a patio, capturing the sun. Warmer in the spring and fall than its surroundings, this microclimate can lengthen the growing season and even provide an environment for plants that might not otherwise survive.

▲ THE UNOBTRUSIVE DARK GREEN LATTICE blends in with the surrounding foliage, while at the same time defining the edge of the patio and forming a visual screen. The square pattern is less busy than the typical diamond-shaped configuration, enhancing the quiet atmosphere.

◄ ALTHOUGH IT'S IMPOSSIBLE to completely screen out the second- and third-floor windows of adjacent buildings, this seating group was placed as close as possible to the wooden fence to maximize the amount of privacy it provides. Replacing the umbrella with a pergola would have increased privacy dramatically but might have changed the corner's tropical feel.

SMALL PATIOS THAT FEEL LARGE

▲ BROAD WALKWAYS AND EXTENSIVE GARDENS dominate this backyard and seem to squeeze the modest seating group off to the side. But, even when seated, people can see over the tops of the plants, and so the small patio area expands by being visually connected to its surroundings.

◄ THROUGH THE ART OF ILLUSION, a trompe l'oeil wall lures you toward this small patio hideaway. Creating a destination spot at the end of a walk is an effective way to carve out a small seating area.

◄ MUCH OF THIS SMALL PATIO is actually the irregular walk, but it doesn't feel that way. Nestled at the bottom of the slope, the patio area is defined by the large rocks and blue planters that mark the entrance.

▲ WHILE IT MAY BE HARD TO FIND even a few minutes to relax, space limitations don't have to get in the way. Cradled in a corner, this small, raised patio is situated perfectly for a quick time-out. The potted plants placed on the steps tie the patio to the lawn nearby, making the patio appear larger than it is.

◄ A SIMPLE WAY TO CREATE A SMALL PATIO is to enlarge one or more sections of a walkway. However, the location should be chosen carefully so that it doesn't feel arbitrary. A good solution is to expand a curve or corner, which affords long views up and down the walk.

Patios as Retreats

IF YOU WANT TO REALLY GET AWAY from it all, consider building a freestanding patio, a retreat that feels isolated from your home. In rural settings that's easy to do, but it's also possible in a large suburban yard—it just takes a little more creativity. Look beyond the obvious. While you can use screening and plantings to shield your patio from the neighbors, you could also build a patio that can only be accessed from a winding path, or tuck your retreat around a corner, out of sight.

When locating the patio and arranging the seating keep in mind that we're most comfortable with our backs against something solid. And position chairs and other seating so that you're looking away from the house, not toward it. Hopefully, with this out-of-sight scenario, the distractions of the house also will be out of mind. As for noise, short of wearing headphones, you won't be able to totally block the sounds around you. A waterfall, fountain, or other gently moving water feature can be a pleasant diversion.

▼ SHADE TREES AND A SMALL POND turn this getaway patio into a sun-dappled oasis. While white might seem an unlikely choice for cushions, today's easy-to-clean fabrics make the option appropriate.

◄ EVEN THOUGH IT'S LOCATED close to the house and a primary walk, this patio feels very private. The tall wooden lattice, with its right angle turn and thick foliage, hides the delicate wrought iron bench from view. The path leading to the alcove is obscured by some overhanging plants.

▼ THIS PATIO APPEARS TO BE a bit open and exposed, but it's the distance that gives this getaway a sense of isolation. Over time, the new plants will grow up and create more of a visual screen.

◄ AN EASY WAY TO CREATE a small retreat is to enlarge the end of a path to be a destination. Surrounding the area with beautiful foliage enhances the setting and makes even the most rudimentary furniture comfortable for a short stay.

▼ SURROUNDED BY TREES and fronting a small patch of green, this patio looks like it's set in a forest clearing. The natural wooden chairs disappear into the background. If not for the white umbrella, the quiet space might go unnoticed.

▲ NOTHING SAYS RETREAT quite as much as an isolated place above the water. Given the gorgeous view of the ocean that's framed by the adjacent trees, these armchairs with pillows are perfect to allow for hours of comfortable reflection.

▲▶ PLANTINGS CAN BE USED TO HELP DEFINE SMALL PATIOS and create a greater sense of remoteness. The knee-high grasses bordering the walk and encircling the pergola (above left) mimic the motion of the swing. The low grouping of plants help separate the small patio from the pea-stone path (above right); over time, the plants will provide more shelter and definition. Plantings used as a central focus make this seating area (right) feel more embedded in the landscape. Plantings used as "grout" between the stones complete the look.

A Standing Stone

A STANDING STONE WILL CREATE A FOCAL POINT in your landscape. You may be able to find a stone on your property; if not, you can buy one from a quarry or masonry supply yard. Be sure to size your stone to your ability to move it (they're heavy!) by rolling or placing it in a garden cart. Very large stones will require the use of a bucket loader or backhoe.

Since standing stones tend to be upright, pick one that has a long profile, not one that is short and squat. At least one-third of the stone will be buried below ground. Make sure you're happy with the form and detail on the part that will show.

STEP 1: **Choose the stone's location, then move the stone close to the spot. Dig a hole a few inches larger than the bottom of the stone and to a depth of one-third the stone's height.**

STEP 2: **To minimize the effects of frost heaving, install a base of about 6 in. to 12 in. of gravel; compact it every few inches with a hand tamper, then install landscape fabric over the top to maintain drainage. (The fabric will prevent soil from migrating into the gravel and plugging it up.)**

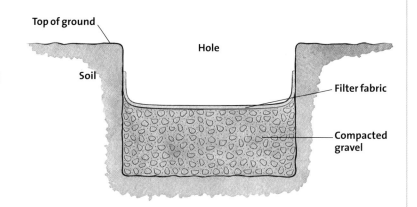

Top of ground

Hole

Soil

Filter fabric

Compacted gravel

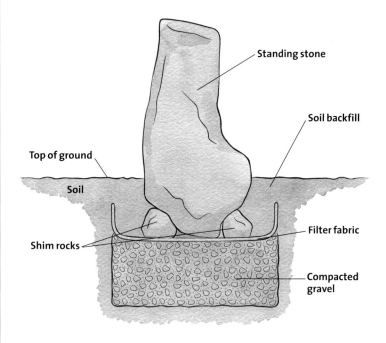

Standing stone

Soil backfill

Top of ground

Soil

Shim rocks

Filter fabric

Compacted gravel

STEP 3: Once the hole has been prepared, tilt the stone into place. Adjust it until it's positioned the way you want it, using smaller shim rocks to prop the stone up if its bottom is uneven. Then fill the rest of the hole with the soil you first took out, compacting it completely with a hand tamper every few inches or so. If the standing stone is in the middle of the patio, finish filling the hole as required for the patio base.

▲ THE PROFUSION OF TALL GRASSES AND BRIGHT BLOSSOMS make a strong visual impact, but there's another important, though more subtle, feature in this scene—the intersection of a square and circle. The pergola, which has a solid roof that protects the cushioned chairs, straddles the round patio, touching it at four places along its circumference.

▲ ALTHOUGH THESE MODERN-LOOKING FOLDING CHAIRS might seem out of place in this natural setting, somehow the contrast works, adding surprise as you walk into the clearing.

▲ THESE WIRE-MESH CHAIRS can easily be pulled together when the conversation calls for hushed voices. Their sled-style legs, which might sit unevenly on a solid patio surface, settle firmly into the pea stone.

▲ ACCESSED BY A NARROW, STEPPING-STONE PATH, this isolated round patio stands out like a red jewel in a green setting. The design of the basket-weave pattern adds style without being overwhelming or too energetic for the serene scene.

▲ THE UMBRELLA FORMED by the forked tree adds intimacy to this secluded patio, and it's hidden by dense foliage along the wooded path.

Water Features

▲ LOCATED AT A TURN IN THE PATH, this pond invites you to stop and pause for a while. The small waterfall at one end adds a little movement to this otherwise tranquil still life.

◄ THIS FOUNTAIN FEATURES CASCADING WATER that adds soothing background noise to the garden. If the fountain had been designed to spray water high into the air, the sound would have been more dramatic, making this feature a focal point.

◄ AN INTEGRAL PART OF PUBLIC SQUARES, fountains also can be an important focal point for the square's smaller cousin, the residential patio. This simple, centrally located fountain is the focus of the seating groups and also can be enjoyed by people as they pass it upon their approach to the patio.

► ENVELOPED IN GREENERY and flanked by two low walls, this patio alcove offers the perfect opportunity to fall under the wall fountain's spell.

▼ THE FAR CORNER OF THIS PATIO is a peaceful haven, perfect for one. The bluestone flagstones are as serene as the pond's surface, and the potted lady's mantel, which has complementary blue foliage, anchors the solitary chair.

PATIOS FOR ONE

▶ SHELTERED BY A ROSE-COVERED PERGOLA, this isolated retreat beckons from the end of a path. The flowers fall across the walk, narrowing it as if to say, "Only one person at a time, please."

▼ SET NEXT TO A SMALL POND, and little more than a clearing amid the flowers, this idyllic spot is an ideal place to unwind. The masses of plantings not only provide texture and color but also attract wildlife.

▲ SOMETIMES YOU WANT A PLACE to be off by yourself where you can read the paper, sip a drink, or just sit and think about nothing. In this comfortable armchair, with its matching end table, there's nothing to bother you except the occasional bee visiting the nearby flowers.

▲ THE HAMMOCK IS THE EPITOME of care-free living. Suspended beneath the whispering trees, this is obviously a place for some serious napping.

Stone Writing Desk

Some creative thinking has transformed an ordinary piece of flagstone into a portable writing desk. A hole was drilled in the thin piece of stone and the top end of the metal bracket secured through it. At the bottom of the bracket, a long clamp is screwed tight, fastening the assembly to the side of the chair.

Patios for Play

ONE WAY TO SHED THE RESPONSIBILITIES of everyday life and recharge those batteries is with a little R and R—rest and relaxation, but many folks prefer the R and P approach—recreation and play. Swimming, playing physical games, or even just horsing around not only burns up calories, but also eases tensions and lets us forget our cares. And of course, providing an outdoor space where children can let off steam benefits both the children and their parents.

Although constructing an indoor space large enough for a swimming pool or basketball court may be beyond the typical budget, that's not true when you're building under the open sky. But instead of just plunking a pool down in the middle of the yard, more and more homeowners are taking a considered approach, integrating patios, pools, and play areas into their landscape, literally turning their backyards into mini-amusement parks.

Big activities can mean big noise, whether it's generated by the entire family splashing around in the pool or a group of neighborhood kids playing a game of tag. So this issue must be addressed when planning a patio for recreation and play. Not only should you think about how noise might impact your neighbors, but you also should consider how it might affect those in your own house—a sleeping baby or someone working in a home office, for example. Try locating the patio away from sensitive areas, or consider creating sound barriers with fences, plantings, or other types of screens.

◀ THE FLOWING LINES OF THIS FREE-FORM POOL and adjacent raised hot tub blend nicely with the surrounding pastoral landscape and echo the curve of the second floor balcony. Positioning the pool off to one side of the backyard leaves plenty of space for a patio.

Patios around Pools

I F YOU STOP AND THINK ABOUT IT, people spend more time sitting around a swimming pool than actually playing in the water. So while the water may be the focal point, the pool's environment and orientation are just as important.

For starters, revise your concept of the area immediately around the pool and imagine transforming that narrow pool "deck" into a full-scale patio. Create generously sized areas where folks can sit and socialize around a table. Although the pool is an activity zone, quiet time is also important. Provide a convenient space for sunbathers to stretch out on chaise lounges or lie down on towels. And think about other amenities you might want to accommodate in your pool-side environment, such as a hot tub, built-in grill, or a snack or drink area.

▲ AN EXPANSIVE CONCRETE-PAVER PATIO dominates this backyard. There's plenty of room for multiple and varied seating arrangements, plus lots of remaining open space. The seating groups are positioned away from the sight line between house and pool, to ensure a clear view of the water from indoors.

◄ LOW RETAINING WALLS carve out just enough space for this brick-surfaced pool patio. Located at the end of the pool area, instead of along the side, the stone steps don't interfere with the seating area, but rather lead directly from the lawn into the pool.

▼ BUILT RIGHT UP TO THE HOUSE, this pool allows someone on the north-facing porch to keep an eagle eye on the water while staying out of the sun. But there's also plenty of room for sun-worshipers to warm up before they take a cooling dip.

◄ THE WORDS INTIMATE AND UNDERSTATED ELEGANCE best describe this tropical-looking pool patio. Square flagstones and grey chairs and lounges blend into the background, allowing the lush foliage to do most of the talking.

▲ THE IVY-COVERED WALL, planting beds, and sinuous edge make this swimming pool feel more like a natural pond. The duck figurines, bird bath, and the solitary wicker chair and otto-man are intentionally clustered together, giving the seating area a sense of place.

► HERE, A BRIGHT WHITE POOL SURROUND and the modern styling of the furniture create a distinct separation between pool area and neighboring landscape.

Positioning a Pool for Sun and View

AS YOU CREATE A DESIGN for your pool and accompanying patio, be sure to orient both with the sun and surrounding view in mind.

- Pools are typically used in the afternoon hours, so they should have a southern to southwestern exposure in most areas of the country, to capture the afternoon sun.

- In hotter climates, you may want to orient the pool so it's shaded a good portion of the day, or at least provide shade with umbrellas or overhead structures.

- Think about what you'd like to see from your pool patio and organize the seating areas accordingly.

- If you don't have a gorgeous distant view, consider sprucing up the landscape around your home and orienting the seating toward the house.

- To create the amount of privacy you desire, screen your pool patio from the neighbors.

◀ IN A TRULY UNIQUE APPROACH to swimming pool design that literally integrates the pool into the landscape, the material that's used to build the stone retaining walls also faces the inside of the pool, to just below the water line. Another thoughtful feature is the generous set of steps that leads into the water.

▲ **WITH THE ADJACENT EVERGREEN TREE** anchoring its position, this four-poster pergola defines the pool-side seating area, effectively making it the focal point of this landscape.

◀ THIS TILE PATIO STRETCHES SEAMLESSLY from the doors of the pool house to the water's edge, making the relatively small area around the pool appear larger. The two seating groups are pushed to the sides of the patio, opening up the middle and clearing the major lines of travel.

▼ ▶ SWIMMING POOLS don't have to be completely surrounded by hard surfaces. Lawns are cooler, softer, and, when walked on, yield underfoot. However, wet feet attract dirt and grass clippings, so incorporating the grass with some stepping stones creates a good mix.

Landscaping around Pools

▲ CONTAINER PLANTS ARE A GREAT WAY to spice up any pool deck, adding color, shape, and texture. One of their great advantages, when compared with fixed planting beds, is that they are portable. Potted plants can be moved around and you can always add more, to create an infinite number of configurations and designs.

▲ THE RUNNING-BOND PATTERN and alternating band of red pavers introduce a sense of movement, making this portion of the pool deck feel like a walkway rather than a place to lie in the sun. This path disappears around a corner, through the potted plants, into a larger, more spacious patio.

▲ INCORPORATING A PLANTING BED and flower pots into a patio scheme helps soften the lines and surfaces of hard materials. These flowers also introduce some color and signal the location of the stairs.

▼ THE PLANTING BEDS that constitute a significant portion of the area around this soaking pool not only provide a natural-canopy screen but also give the impression that the pool was shaped to conform to the vegetation.

▲ BIG, RUGGED, AND BOLDLY COLORED, the irregular flagstones that comprise this large pool-and-hot-tub deck have the visual strength to stand up to the surrounding landscape. A more refined material probably would have been swallowed up by the towering pine trees.

▲ MUCH OF THE BEAUTY of this carefully designed infinity-edge pool is created by emphasizing the contrast between its sharp, rectangular lines and the soft edges and blended colors of the surrounding plantings.

▲ THIS POOL DECK IS PAVED with square-cut flagstones that were finished with a honed, not polished, surface. The same stone material is used at the edge of the pool and makes the deck look like a smooth carpet that extends from the pool house to the water.

► THE STUDIED PLACEMENT OF LARGE ROCKS, the pool surround's undulating edge, and the light-colored concrete pavers all work in concert to create the illusion that this pool deck is a sandy ocean-side beach.

Pool Decking Options

THE AREA THAT SURROUNDS an in-ground swimming pool is called the deck. Next to the size, shape, and orientation of the pool itself, the deck is perhaps the most important consideration when planning a swimming pool. When deciding which material to use, keep a few things in mind:

- Materials installed closer to the pool, where people walk barefoot, should be easy on the feet and not be slippery when wet.

- Pool decks can get hot, but light-colored materials that reflect the sun won't get as hot as darker ones.

- The constant exposure to water and, in northern areas of the country, freeze/thaw cycles, is hard on pool decks, so materials should be durable. Low-cost materials may be attractive in the beginning, but they may not be a good value over the long term.

There are a number of choices and each has its advantages and disadvantages:

- **POURED-IN-PLACE CONCRETE** is a popular choice, both for its affordability and design flexibility. The typical monotone grey finish is a thing of the past because concrete can be colored, stamped, broom finished, or have an exposed aggregate finish. Cracking and freezing can cause problems in cold climates.

- **BRICK OR CONCRETE PAVERS** offer numerous colors, styles, and installation patterns. Although typically more expensive than poured concrete, pavers are very durable; plus individual pavers are easy to remove and replace if damaged. Pool decks made of pavers can easily be expanded to create a pool-side patio.

- **NATURAL STONE,** in the form of flagstones or pavers, makes a very durable decking material but is usually more expensive than other options. Available in a wide range of colors, stone adds a natural aesthetic to your pool deck and is compatible with any architectural style, whether you choose informal, irregular flagstones or more formal, regular flagstones or pavers.

- **CERAMIC TILE** is also a popular choice for pool decks, but because glazed tiles are slippery, only unglazed tiles are appropriate. Installed over a concrete base, tile is a relatively costly, but beautiful, alternative. Over time, the grout joints can spall, or crack, requiring repairs that might be difficult to blend in with existing joints.

▶ IRREGULAR FLAGSTONES top this pool-side hot tub. Instead of trying to make the joints disappear, white grout was chosen to emphasize the angular nature of the stone and match the diagonal white tile on the tub's facing.

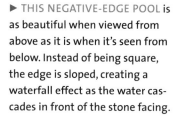
▲ THE POOL HOUSE AND WOODEN PERGOLA offer refuge from the midday sun and, shielded from the driveway by a tall stucco wall, there's enough privacy for pool-side dining in bathing suits.

▶ THIS NEGATIVE-EDGE POOL is as beautiful when viewed from above as it is when it's seen from below. Instead of being square, the edge is sloped, creating a waterfall effect as the water cascades in front of the stone facing.

Blending a Patio, Walkway, and Wall

One of the advantages of building walkways, retaining walls, and patios with concrete pavers and wall blocks is that it's easy to achieve a coordinated look without risking being bland. The variation in color creates interest, while the textural difference between pavers installed flat and those installed on edge provides detailing. There are dozens of colors and styles of pavers and blocks to choose from and myriad installation patterns.

▼ REFLECTING OFF THE WATER'S SURFACE, lights installed in the ceiling of this patio roof appear to be candles floating on top of the pool. The effect, combined with the free-form step leading into the water, sets a dramatic scene.

▲ THIS VIEW FROM UNDER THE THATCHED ROOF reveals that the retaining walls and steps down to the water are actually a part of the pool deck. One wall is large enough for sunbathing, others create planters or surfaces on which to display potted plants, while still others form a perfect place to sit.

Patios for Sports and Recreation

I F THEY HAD THE NECESSARY SKILLS and opportunity to do so, children would create outdoor play areas that include things most adults might not consider—bugs, plants, water, sand. These elements engage children's imaginations and are things they can manipulate, providing opportunities for discovery and free play. Keep this in mind, and consider including your children in the creation of your play-area patio.

Young children prefer to play closer to home, perhaps within site of a door. As they grow and become more independent they will probably want some privacy, which you can create with taller fencing or other screening. It's obvious that neatness does not typically come easy to children, and one of the advantages of playing outdoors is permitting them to be messy. If a play patio is connected with an adult area you can keep the mess contained by using low walls, fences, or other edgings. Providing storage also will help, either in a nearby garage or by using a waterproof toy storage box or one that can be rolled to a protected spot.

Of course playtime is not limited to young children, or even to children at all. As a part of a larger patio you might include a horseshoe pit, putting green, or even a half-court basketball court for the child in all of us.

► SEPARATED FROM the adult-oriented dining patio by a low concrete-block wall and metal fence, this well-appointed play area is close enough to keep an eye on the children, but far enough away so they're not yelling in your ear.

▼ IF YOU'RE A REAL BASKETBALL ENTHUSIAST perhaps it's time to remove that hoop from in front of the garage and build a court where you can really strut your stuff. A half-size court takes up less space than you might think and can be integrated into an adjacent patio.

▼ PLAYING THIS OVERSIZED GAME of chess exercises the body as well as the mind, giving a whole new meaning to "hands-on experience." Of course younger children, or those wanting to do something less taxing, can always replace the chess pieces with super-sized checkers.

Play It Safe

WHILE PHYSICAL ACTIVITY is important for the health and development of children, there are dangers that go along with outdoor play. Every year about 50,000 children are taken to hospital emergency rooms for injuries associated with home playground equipment. Fortunately, there are a number of measures you can take to reduce the risk of injury.

- **SUPERVISION:** Never leave young children unsupervised in a play area.

- **LINE OF SIGHT:** Make sure there is a direct line of sight from the house to the play area.

- **AGE APPROPRIATENESS:** Choose play equipment that is appropriate for the age of the children who will use it.

- **PROPER CLEARANCE:** Provide the proper amount of clearance between pieces of play equipment and from obstacles such as trees and buildings. Locate the play area away from grills, fire pits, and other dangerous places.

- **CORRECT CONSTRUCTION MATERIALS:** Use materials that are rust- or rot-resistant or treated with environmentally safe preservatives. Make sure there are no protruding bolts or screws that could potentially cause injuries.

- **PROPER ANCHORING:** Make sure swing sets and climbable structures are securely anchored to the ground.

- **SUITABLE SURFACE:** Install surface materials that are suitable for the type of play—smooth, gap-fee surfaces where trikes and Big Wheels® will be driven, and loose-fill, impact-absorbing materials under swings and climbable equipment, where children are above the ground.

◄ THE AREA BELOW AND AROUND play and climbable structures should be relatively soft and able to cushion a child in the event of a fall. Install a 6-in.- to 12-in.-thick layer of materials such as bark and rubber mulch, pea stone, or fine play-sand. To help keep down the weeds, put a layer of landscape fabric between the ground and the play surface.

▼ ACKNOWLEDGING THAT CHILDREN just love to have fun in the dirt, this play patio is a child's dream come true. The large rocks can serve as an obstacle course one minute and the next, a tall cliff that just has to be conquered. And off in a distant corner, the log cabin offers a place to hide or play quietly.

Sunken Sandbox

EVEN WITH ALL OF THE HIGH-TECH and sleek plastic toys available, children are still drawn to the tried-and-true sandbox. They can spend hours digging, burying, sifting, moving, and shaping. Building a sandbox is relatively easy, and it's a valuable addition to any patio.

Composite landscaping timbers, made with recycled plastic, are an excellent material, since they are smooth, stable, and won't splinter or rot. They're also very heavy, so once they're secured in place they stay put.

STEP 1: **Choose a spot for the sandbox, keeping in mind sun and shade, then dig out the soil. Excavate the hole to about 2 ft. larger than the perimeter of the sandbox, and make it the depth of two timbers stacked on top of each other. Line the bottom of the hole with landscape fabric.**

STEP 2: **Arrange the bottom course of timbers in the hole, butting the ends against one another. Level each timber by digging out or adding more soil as required. Make sure the frame is square by measuring the lengths of the diagonals (they should equal one another), and adjust the timbers as necessary until the diagonals are the proper length. Using galvanized metal angle brackets and decking screws, fasten the four inside corners of the timbers together. The holes for the screws may have to be predrilled. Carefully backfill around the perimeter of the timbers, compacting with a hand tamper so that the earth locks the frame in place.**

STEP 3: **Next, arrange the top course of timbers on top of the bottom course, alternating the joints and aligning the top timbers so the sides are flush with the bottom course. Using galvanized metal plates and decking screws, fasten the top course together and to the bottom course. Backfill, as in Step 2, so that the ground is flush with the top of the timbers.**

STEP 4: **Finally, fill the sandbox with between 6 in. and 10 in. of clean play-sand. The top row of timbers provides a convenient seat for the kids.**

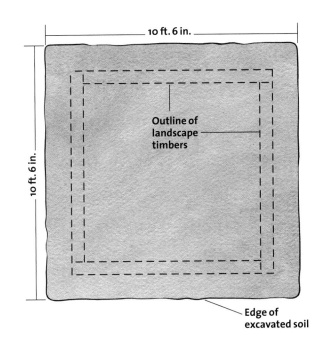

10 ft. 6 in.

10 ft. 6 in.

Outline of landscape timbers

Edge of excavated soil

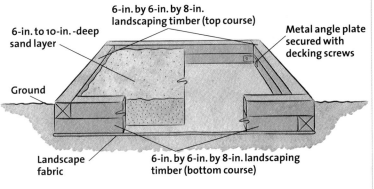

6-in. by 6-in. by 8-in. landscaping timber (top course)

6-in. to 10-in.-deep sand layer

Metal angle plate secured with decking screws

Ground

Landscape fabric

6-in. by 6-in. by 8-in. landscaping timber (bottom course)

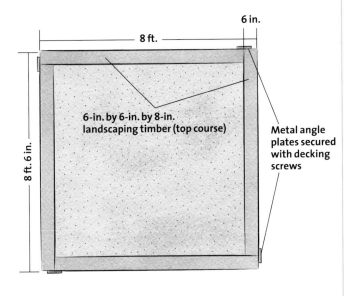

8 ft.

6 in.

8 ft. 6 in.

6-in. by 6-in. by 8-in. landscaping timber (top course)

Metal angle plates secured with decking screws

Creating an Outdoor Environment for Kids

GENERALLY SPEAKING, CHILDREN PREFER something wild and diverse rather than orderly and predictable in their outdoor play areas. Think beyond manufactured play structures and include natural items such as logs, rocks, and "found" items that encourage children to exercise their imaginations as well as their bodies. Here are some components to consider:

- Water, whether it's available at a nearby spigot or brought close with a hose
- Sand, particularly when it can be mixed with water
- Places and features to lean on, hide in, or sit in, on, or under
- Structures, equipment, and materials that can be changed and manipulated by children

- Different levels, nooks, and crannies
- Vegetation, including trees, bushes, flowers, and long grasses
- Creatures, such as bugs and small animals that might be attracted to small, constructed ponds
- Shade

◄ ASIDE FROM THE FULLY appointed play structure, there are less obvious features that help make this children's area a success—the circular concrete walk, which provides a smooth trike-riding surface, and the out-of-the-way bench, where adults can sit and keep a discrete eye on the little gymnasts.

▼ WHO SAYS GARDENING has to be all work? This small patio, with its chaise lounge and side table, provides a place to take a well-earned break. If children are part of the workforce, the plant teepee, especially when it's covered with climbing beans, offers the same for them.

▲ TENNIS COURTS, because of
their size, can be an overwhelming presence in some backyards.
The large trees and tall evergreen
hedge that surround this court
help minimize its impact; the
hedge also affords some protection on windy days.

◄ ALTHOUGH PRACTICING
GOLF'S long-distance shots
at home is out of the question,
not so the fine art of putting.
The serene environment that
surrounds this putting green is
sure to help calm the nerves
and steady the hand so the golfer
strikes the ball just right.

► POOL TABLES are usually associated with dark, indoor spaces, their green surfaces lit by pendant lights hung with metal shades. However, all-weather pool tables, made from materials that can stand up to the elements, shed a whole new light on the subject.

◄ THIS PALAPA, a traditional umbrella made from palm fronds or other natural materials, offers a shady spot to rest between games or sets, and it might even make you feel like you're vacationing in the Caribbean.

Front Entries and Driveways

W ITH ALL THE TIME, ATTENTION, AND MONEY that's lavished on new kitchens, master suites, and great-room additions, all intended to turn modern-day houses into homes, there's one important feature that's often ignored—transitional spaces, such as front entries and driveways. After all, there's something to be said for that old "home is a castle" metaphor. Even with all of the modern conveniences, we still want our homes to be sanctuaries, places where we can detach from the outside world and just be ourselves.

The experience of entering a house actually influences the way you feel once you're inside. If the entrance into the house is too abrupt, there is no sense of arrival. Transitional spaces, however, provide a distinct signal to someone approaching and entering your home that says they are moving from the public environment to a more protected, private world.

Creating well-defined transitional areas is about establishing and emphasizing change. Altering the material underfoot, direction of travel, and view along the way are key transitional elements. Marking those changes with gates and arches, or altering the sense of scale by enclosing spaces with fences, walls, covered walks, or arbors also helps create effective transitional spaces.

◄ ACCESSING A FRONT DOOR that is located one floor above the driveway can be challenging. Here, terraced stone walls reduce the perceived height of the adjacent hillside and carve out space for the wide, welcoming steps.

Front Entry Areas

WHEN ASKED TO IMAGINE an historic, picturesque neighborhood, you might envision a quiet street where white picket fences frame each front yard, and walkways begin at the sidewalk and, sheltered by tall shade trees, lead to deep front porches.

Contrast that with the image of a typical subdivision home, where the front lawn runs in an uninterrupted green swath from the house right into the street. While it may not be possible, or perhaps desirable, to replicate the past, recreating the sense of a warm and welcoming front entry is a wise investment—and it's relatively easy to do.

A front entry must relate to the front door. But as you work through your design options, keep in mind that a front entry can, as in houses of old, encompass much more space than just a few square feet in front of the door. Don't be afraid to sacrifice your front lawn; consider giving all or most of it over to your new outdoor entry. Take style cues from your home and work with the contours of your property to create an approach that's functional and beautiful.

▲ **THIS CHARMING FRONT ENTRY,** framed by climbing ivy, is all the more inviting thanks to the semicircular entry patio, with its edge-defining hedge, step up, and change in material from the walkway.

▶ **A WELL-DESIGNED ENTRY** protects visitors from the elements as they wait at the door to be let in. Although shallow, the overhang that shelters this front entry and top step is wide enough to protect several people at once.

▲ IF AN ENTRY DOOR can't be easily seen as it's approached, it's important to provide visual clues for visitors, to assure them that they're going in the right direction. With the approach from the side along a clear-finished wood wall, the bright red paint attracts attention, indicating that something important (the door) is ahead.

▲ **THE FIRST FLOOR** of this brick home is quite high above the ground. Rather than bridge that distance with a set of steps alone, the homeowners decided to expand things a bit. This entry patio reduces the apparent vertical distance between ground and porch floor, making the house feel accessible and integrated with its surroundings.

▲ COLUMNS HAVE BEEN USED to mark entryways and transition spaces for centuries, and they remain popular today. When used alone or in pairs they should be large enough to project a substantial presence, as they do here.

▲ RATHER THAN LEADING YOU directly to the front door, this walkway takes a turn or two, slowing you down so you can enjoy the beautiful stonework. The narrow walk opens up onto an entry patio that's hidden just behind the flower beds.

▼ THE IRREGULAR-FLAGSTONE WALK, simple wooden bench, rustic hand-rail, and even the plantings all combine to create a country-style entry.

Simple Touches Define an Entry

◄ FOR EMPHASIS, transition points are often denoted with a visually arresting feature. Although this short, rough stone pillar is not unusual, the addition of the sharply contrasting smooth sphere makes the composition stand out.

▼ CAREFUL ATTENTION TO COLOR makes this entry successful. Because the adjacent surface is painted a darker color, the bright white wall jumps out of the shadows, making it easy to find the front door.

◄ EVEN IN THE DAYTIME, this whimsical arrangement of colorful lanterns enlivens the front walkway. By night they cast enough light to see the walk.

▲ THIS NICELY DETAILED WOODEN ARCH, which will eventually be covered with climbing vines, interjects a bit of ceremony into what otherwise would be a relatively plain entrance to this simple home.

◄ SET UNDER A PROTECTIVE OVERHANG, this built-in bench is welcoming and provides a spot for reading the mail or taking off shoes. The power pole at the beginning of the walkway has been transformed into a support for a climbing rose.

► INSTEAD OF USING COLOR, subtle changes in texture signify the entrance to this southwestern-style home. Wide, welcoming flagstone steps stretch into the pea-stone driveway and are flanked by walls built of rough-cut stone.

▲ VIEWED FROM THE BEGINNING of this brick walkway, the house is partially screened by some strategically located plantings, but the front door is clearly visible. The gentle curve encourages those approaching the house to slow down and enjoy the surroundings.

► THIS SIMPLE BREEZEWAY ROOF is in keeping with the Cape-style home. The columns break the space under the breezeway into three distinct sections and frame two views—one, close up, of the tree, and one into the distance.

▲ SOLID FENCES are an obvious and relatively inex-
pensive way to create complete privacy. However, a tall,
unadorned wooden fence can present an unfriendly,
fort-like impression. Not so with this flower-covered
fence, which welcomes visitors with a burst of color.

◄ RECTANGULAR SHAPES DOMINATE the entrance
to this modern-style home. The orientation of the
large, concrete stepping stones influences the
approach to the house: walking perpendicularly to
their width tends to slow things down; after turning
the corner, the visitor can move along at a faster clip.

◄ ENTERING THIS HOME is marked by ceremony, as the walkway directs you around the edges of a formal, symmetrical garden. Pairs of trees and pillars at the opening in the brick wall signal a change. Beyond, the right-angle turns give way to a sweeping curve that whisks you to the door.

► POURED-IN-PLACE CONCRETE, when installed appropriately, can be a successful part of a nicely detailed entry. This concrete walkway and patio was colored a rich red to complement the home's brick facade. The expansion joints, a requirement of any poured concrete installation, are an integral part of the design and not just a necessity.

QUICK AND EASY HOW-TO

Small Fountain

FOR A MINIMAL INVESTMENT OF TIME AND MONEY you can build a small fountain and bring the soothing sounds of falling water into your garden or patio. This simple fountain is comprised of five components—a plastic, bowl-like pond liner, submersible water pump, plastic flower pot, galvanized hardware cloth, and a surround made of wedge-shaped concrete pavers. Choose pavers that, when laid out side by side, create an inner circle with a diameter equal to the diameter of the pool liner.

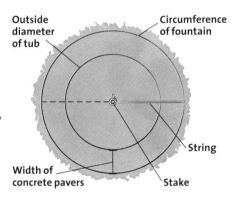

Outside diameter of tub

Circumference of fountain

String

Width of concrete pavers

Stake

STEP 1: Locate where the center of the fountain will be and put a stake there. Then, using a string fastened to the stake that's equal to the fountain's radius, mark the outside circumference of the finished fountain. Next, dig out the circle 2 in. deep and fill the hole with 2 in. of clean sand. (If you live in a region subject to frost or freezing, make the hole 8 in. to 14 in. deep and install 6 in. to 12 in. of crushed gravel below the sand.) Then position the pond liner in the center so that it is stable and level.

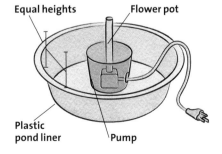

Equal heights

Flower pot

Plastic pond liner

Pump

STEP 2: Choose a flower pot that's as tall as the pool liner is deep. Cut a hole in the side of the pot that is large enough to feed the pump cord through, slip the pump inside the pot, and put the pot-pump assembly on the bottom of the liner, trailing the cord over the top of the liner. With a pair of tin snips, cut the hardware cloth to create a circle that's the same size as the liner. Cut a hole in the center of the cloth large enough to pull the pump through. Make a notch in the side of the hardware cloth for the cord, and set the hardware cloth on top of the liner.

◄ WHETHER THEY'RE INSTALLED across a front walk or integrated into a garden path, wooden arches are an easy way to add a special touch to your landscape. They are available in many different styles and can be outfitted with gates and built-in seating.

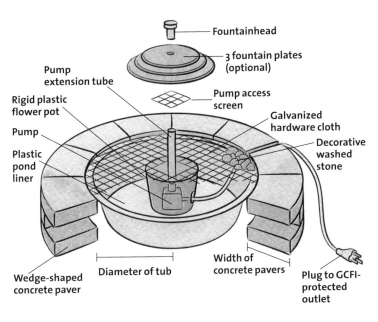

Fountainhead

3 fountain plates (optional)

Pump extension tube

Pump access screen

Rigid plastic flower pot

Galvanized hardware cloth

Pump

Decorative washed stone

Plastic pond liner

Wedge-shaped concrete paver

Diameter of tub

Width of concrete pavers

Plug to GCFI-protected outlet

STEP 3: Stack the concrete pavers around the tub, making the surround at least one course higher than the liner. Cover the top of the hardware cloth with decorative, washed stone. Finally, install the fountainhead, fill the liner with water, and plug the fountain in. For an optional feature, drill a hole in the center of one or more ceramic dishes and install them over the pump shaft. This will create a small, cascading pool effect.

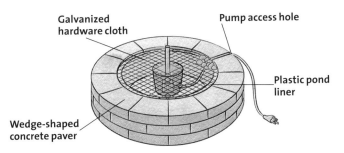

Galvanized hardware cloth

Pump access hole

Plastic pond liner

Wedge-shaped concrete paver

▲ FRONTED BY STRIKING VEGETATION, this brick wall and arch are impressive, but there's another important part of this entry that may go unnoticed. The pea-stone walk is a lighter, contrasting color and softer underfoot than brick, which makes the entry wall more prominent.

Drainage in a Walkway

AFTER HEAVY RAINS, puddles can form in low spots in walkways that are constructed with tight-fitting, impervious materials or over poor-draining soil. Installing drains can alleviate this problem. Typically, walkway drains are connected to 4-in. PVC piping which, if the grade permits, is pitched "to daylight" or to a below-grade drywell made of washed stone.

▲ BEGINNING AT RIGHT ANGLES TO THE HOME, this entry stair traverses the slope and then turns to face the front door. Utilizing brick for the retaining walls and steps and painting the railing white to match the house trim creates an integrated look. The post light is situated to illuminate the steps.

▲ ALTHOUGH A ROOF is an important entryway feature, it will block out a lot of light. Not so with this translucent-roof shelter, which protects the front entry from the elements without darkening it.

◀ IN AN INTERESTING TWIST, the standard basket-weave pattern used in this walkway is turned 45 degrees and flows toward the house. The thickets of flowers bordering the path escort visitors to the front door.

ENTRY COURTYARDS

▶ LOCATED RIGHT NEXT to a busy street, the high stucco walls and solid wooden gate provide a much needed barrier. The sun- and flower-filled courtyard encourages you to leave your cares outside.

◀ COURTYARDS DON'T have to be elaborate to be successful. A simple, white picket fence creates a perfect courtyard for this traditional-style home. Chairs placed near the entry offer a view across the courtyard and to the flowers and gate.

Naturalistic Courtyard

By using locally available materials you can create a naturalistic landscape that blends in and harmonizes with its surroundings. Another important feature is to create a plan that doesn't look like it's been designed but rather has occurred naturally. Native plants, which require less maintenance, add a final touch and complete the scene.

▲ ENTRY COURTYARDS ARE PATIOS that are enclosed on all sides with definite boundaries, such as walls, fences, buildings, or thick hedges. Courtyards don't have to create complete privacy; in fact, views to the adjacent surroundings can be desirable. Seating, plantings, and sculpture all help courtyards come alive and make the trip to the front door truly memorable.

◄ THIS FORMAL COURTYARD with its large gate, pond, playful statues, and intricate brick walkway has an old-world flavor. All of these features can easily be incorporated on a smaller, more affordable scale.

Fountains in the Landscape

▶ FOUNTAINS REPRESENT the source of life. The ever-mesmerizing flow of water and a fountain's peaceful sounds have been a part of cities and homes for centuries. Part of the beauty of this brick fountain is the rhythmic pattern established by the three nesting half-circles—the water spout, fountain pool, and brick walkway.

▶ IN HOT CLIMATES, fountains have a psychologically cooling effect, which people sitting in the shade of this front porch would appreciate. If things get really warm, the square-stone wall forming the fountain pool is just the right height to sit on to dip a hand in the water.

▲ THE ENTRY TO THIS HOME is elegantly marked by a modest stone pillar and simple three-head fountain. Beautiful circular patterns, which might have gone unnoticed but for the falling leaves, decorate the surface of the water.

◄ SURROUNDED BY a canopy of trees, this bubbling stone fountain is perfectly suited to its setting, which looks very much like a jungle clearing. The patio, a mosaic of irregular flagstones, enhances the wild feeling.

Driveways

PERHAPS THE DEMISE OF THE TRADITIONAL FRONT ENTRY can be blamed on the automobile. Our commuter lifestyle has allowed families to make friends and find playmates who live across town, not just across the street. And so, instead of strolling down the sidewalks, most folks arrive at our houses by car, in our driveways. Disembarking in front of the garage, which is typically close to the side door, guests slip into the service entrance and the front door is abandoned—seldom, if ever, used.

If you want your front door to come to life again, then you need to showcase it to create the feeling of a front entry. Begin by deflecting attention away from other doors. Establish a clear, easily accessible entrance by utilizing features such as gates, columns, and plantings. Because the driveway surface is so large, it dominates the visual field, so think about a distinct change of material to separate the entry from the parking area.

If you're lucky enough to have the space, you might consider carving out a pull-out area where guests can park before they reach the garage. Not only does this prevent parked cars from blocking yours in the garage, but it also makes your guests, who now have a place intended only for them, feel important.

▶ DUE TO SPACE CONSTRAINTS, this asphalt driveway is only a short distance away from the side of the house, but a well-thought-out design, beautifully executed, makes the best of the situation. Instead of just a narrow flight of stairs, a broad flagstone step and wooden landing were constructed the full length of the house, clearly separating the entry from the drive and creating more useable space.

▲ THIS NATURAL-FINISH WOOD PERGOLA grabs attention and helps visitors locate the way in, via the stepping-stone path. The arms that support the roof structure are cantilevered out from posts that are set well back from the driveway, out of harm's way.

▲ THE EDGES OF ASPHALT DRIVEWAYS are usually vague and ill-defined. While stone and asphalt curbs do address that issue, they can be damaged during snow removal and may be a tripping hazard. This border of concrete pavers is a great solution, giving a finished look and framing the flower beds.

▶ BECAUSE GARAGES AND DRIVEWAYS are often large, adjacent landscaping has to be appropriately sized to be effective. A low flowerbed would get lost next to this garage, but, with the archway's help, the newly planted evergreen trees are large enough even now to define the entry.

▲ CONSTRUCTED WITH IRREGULAR FLAGSTONES that are similar in color and texture to the shingled house, this driveway complements the landscape and looks like a large patio. Framed by sculptural tree trunks, a simple stone walk leads through the wall to the front door.

▼ THE FLAT ROOF OF THIS GARAGE has been turned into an entry patio that guests access by climbing the stone steps. Steps this steep and long are safer with a handrail along at least one side.

▲ MULTIPLE LAYERS HAVE BEEN USED to create the approach to this modest bungalow. Landscaping timbers, deep planting beds, and a white picket fence form a gradual transition that nevertheless separates the parking area from the path and yard.

Small Things Make the Difference

Asphalt, although certainly an appropriate and serviceable material to use for driveways, doesn't have a lot of visual appeal or character. A little attention to detail can change that. Here, instead of installing the asphalt right up to the garage, a substantial brick boarder crisply defines and dresses up the edge of the driveway.

▼ LARGE EXPANSES OF IMPERVIOUS SURFACES, such as asphalt and concrete, present environmental concerns by inhibiting groundwater recharge and creating storm-water runoff problems. Gridded pavers, like those used in this driveway, are made with holes that allow water to seep into the ground.

Moving Through the Landscape

ALTHOUGH YOU CERTAINLY WANT your home to provide protection and privacy for your family, you also want easy ways to access and enjoy the surrouding areas. By effectively employing two elements—walkways and steps—you'll remove impediments and be able to use, and move freely through, your landscape, no matter what the terrain.

Walkways and steps, of course, make it possible to move from driveway to front door or from back door to outdoor play patio—but there's more to them than the line from Point A to Point B. Your landscape's paths have a sensory component as well. Features that delight and capture the eye, the ear, and the sense of smell are important and should be considered integral to the design and construction of walkways and steps.

When planning your travel network, it's quite likely you'll need more than one walkway and at least one set of steps, so keep a few things in mind. Start with the big picture. Before you focus in on the details, determine how your walks and stairs will be used and get an overall sense of their location and size. Then, consider multiple options. Even though it's often chosen in the end, don't get stuck with the first design. By coming up with several alternatives you'll be assured you've not missed an opportunity or better solution. Be ready for compromise. The perfect plan is rare, if not an impossibility, in the world of construction.

◄ THIS SINUOUS AND SMOOTH BRICK WALKWAY sidles up to the front door. Although the door is hidden from view, the well-articulated walk imparts a sense of confidence that the visitor is going in the right direction.

Walkways

WHILE WALKWAYS CAN BE identified as primary, secondary, or tertiary depending on their purpose and relative size, it's also possible to categorize them by the installation methods and materials used to construct them: solid carpet, loose fill, stepping stone, or mixed materials. Using both categorizations acknowledges that it's possible to make a primary, secondary, or tertiary walkway from different materials and helps you choose the appropriate material for a particular walkway.

Solid-carpet walkways have small joints and are typically constructed with brick or concrete pavers, flagstones, tile, or poured concrete. This type of walk usually provides a smooth surface and stable footing. Loose-fill walkways can be made with a number of materials, such as washed stone, bark mulch, and brick chips. Softer underfoot, these materials can get stuck in shoe soles (or even get right into your shoes), and may need to be replenished from time to time. "Stepping stone" is somewhat of a misnomer, because in addition to stones, wood rounds or pads made from concrete, wood, or pavers also can be used to create this type of walkway. And, as the name suggests, mixed-material paths combine two or more materials.

▼ RUGGED ONE-PIECE STEPS dominate the gardens in front of this low-slung bungalow. The visual weight of the steps and retaining wall adds substance to the house and helps balance the powerful effect of the large tree.

▲ STEPPING-STONE PATHS are a good choice for informal landscapes. Large stepping stones, while they may require the help of heavy equipment to install, provide safe footing, particularly when they are positioned to allow grass to grow between them.

◄ THIS LOOSE-FILL WALKWAY appears to be a slow-moving stream, an effect that is enhanced by the flat, dark stone border. Halfway up the walk the stones jut out, forming a point around which the "stream" flows.

▼ RESEMBLING A LARGE FOOTPRINT, this meandering tertiary path steps off from the side of the front walk. The unruly stepping stones are an effective contrast to the carefully controlled concrete walk and steps.

▲ THIS CLASSIC BRICK WALKWAY, created in a running-bond pattern, adds a twist—it's edged with bricks that are vertically placed. The flair at the end of the walk welcomes guests to the lawn.

◄ MIXING DIFFERENT TYPES OF MATERIALS from the same color family adds visual interest. The different shapes and textures of the irregular flagstones, smooth oval stones, and poured concrete in this walkway result in a harmonious composition.

▲ THIS SOLID-CARPET walkway is constructed with flagstones installed in an unusual stacked pattern in which all of the joints align. Inlaid bricks add an unexpected element.

▲ WASHED STONE is not only sorted by size, but sometimes by color, too. The walkway here is complemented by the variety of green tones in the plantings, with a few areas of color adding visual relief.

Path Materials

A WIDE RANGE OF MATERIALS can be used for constructing paths and walls. Because the choices are so numerous and the same material often is referred to by more than one name, it can get confusing. The following list will help you understand the broad categories so that communicating with contractors and suppliers is easier.

- **PAVERS:** Pavers are generally considered to be relatively small. Although they come in many sizes and shapes, the typical paver is the size of a standard brick—approximately 4 in. wide, 8 in. long, and 2 in. thick. Pavers can be made from brick, concrete, tile, or stone.

- **FLAGSTONES:** Flagstones can be sorted into two general categories—irregular and regular. Irregular, or natural, flagstones come in a variety of shapes—rectangles, triangles, parallelograms—and have uneven edges. Regular, or dimension, flagstones are cut to precise shapes, typically squares and rectangles, and have finished edges. Flagstones are larger and thinner than pavers, ranging in thickness from 1 in. to 4 in., and from 12 in. to 36 in. or more in length and width. Most flagstones are some type of stone, but they also can be made from precast concrete.

- **LOOSE-FILL MATERIALS:** Loose-fill materials can be grouped into two categories—soft and hard types. Soft loose materials include bark mulch, wood chips, pine needles, and nut hulls, while washed stone, seashells, brick chips, and recycled glass with smoothed edges are examples of hard materials. Loose-fill materials are relatively easy to install, but they must be replenished from time to time, because soft types rot or blow away, and hard types get embedded in the ground or are swept away.

- **WASHED STONE:** Washed stone is produced at a gravel pit and separated from sand and soil by being washed with water. Washed stone is graded according to size, 3/8 in. to 1 in. Pea stone, which frequently is used for paths, is 3/8 in. in size.

- **CAST-IN-PLACE CONCRETE:** Cast-in-place concrete is mixed at a plant, delivered to the site in a truck, and poured into forms. Because it begins as a liquid, cast-in-place concrete can be formed into different shapes, such as curves, relatively easily. As it hardens it can be troweled, bushed, or washed to create a variety of surface textures. It also can be embedded with stones, tiles, or other small items to create beautiful designs.

- **FIELDSTONE:** Fieldstones are various types of native stone found in fields and woods. They vary in shape and size depending on the region of the country. Fieldstones can be used to build walls, and stones with at least one flat surface can be used for paths and steps.

- **INTERLOCKING CONCRETE BLOCK:** Specially formulated for exposure and outdoor use, precast, interlocking concrete blocks are used to build walls and steps. They come in a wide variety of shapes, surface finishes, and colors.

- **VENEER BRICK:** Veneer brick is formulated for outdoor use and is typically used to cover up regular concrete blocks or poured concrete, to provide a finished surface on freestanding or retaining walls.

- **LANDSCAPING TIMBERS:** In spite of their name, landscaping timbers don't have to be made from wood. With the advent of recycled plastic, landscaping timbers also are made from composite materials (a combination of wood and plastic) or just plastic. Wood timbers should either be made from rot-resistant species or be treated with an approved wood preservative. Landscaping timbers can be 4x4, 6x6, or 8x8 and are typically 8 ft. long.

◄ LOOSE FILL MATERIALS are easy to manipulate, and as evidenced by this pea-stone walk, allow an otherwise straight path to assume an undulating edge. The plantings that border this pea-stone walk pinch in, narrowing the path at several points. Changing the look of the path simply requires moving the vegetation or introducing additional plants.

Inlay Designs

▼ REMINISCENT OF A MIXED-MEDIA COLLAGE, this attention-grabbing detail combines brick pavers, flagstones, small round stones, and a custom-made tile leaf. Details such as these can be inserted directly into the middle of a walkway or can be placed more discretely, off to the side, as was done here.

▲ THIS PLAYFUL DESIGN demonstrates one of the many opportunities of working with poured concrete. In this case, broken pieces of blue tile were pressed into the wet, colored concrete. Although the process was labor intensive, the results are worth the work.

◄ A QUILTED BLOCK OF CERAMIC TILES was popped into the brick portion of this solid-carpet walk. The square block was custom-made, taking into account the width of the joints between the brick; each was designed to be exactly three bricks wide.

▲ THE HERRINGBONE PATTERN of this brick walkway gives it a formal feeling, which is amplified by the almost ceremonial placement of the pair of large, high-backed wooden benches.

◄ ALTHOUGH THEY ARE LARGE, these simple stepping stones recede into the background, keeping the focus on the custom-made metal gate. Since the shape and scale of the stones and gate are similar, the light piercing the gate and the surrounding view take on more importance.

SOLID-CARPET WALKWAYS

▲ THIS WALK HAS AN OLD WORLD FEEL that's created by
the mixed size, multicolored concrete pavers, skillfully chosen
to echo the colors of the stones in the walls. The wandering
walls widen to form a small piazza and are just the right
height for sitting.

◄ AN OTHERWISE SEDATE SOLID-CARPET WALKWAY is
interspersed with small, square tile pavers that spice things
up and create a bit of design tension. Bands of color add more
punch than if individual red tiles were placed randomly.

▲ PLANNING A PATIO AND WALKWAY simultaneously will allow you to create a cohesive design. The concrete pavers of this raised patio are lighter in color than those of the walk, separating the two areas, while the gray granite steps are tied into the patio and walkway with edging of the same material.

◄ A LARGE PIECE OF IRREGULAR FLAGSTONE acts like a threshold, leading onto this solid-carpet walk. The mix of colors—reds and grays—reflects the different shades of brick used on the exterior of the house.

Lighting the Way

▲ STRATEGICALLY LOCATED at each short flight of steps, these spotlights will cast a bright light when the sun goes down, making the stairs safe.

▲ THIS FLIGHT OF STAIRS is relatively long for steps that lead to a front door, but each tread is easy to see since they are individually lit. The wall-mounted lantern highlights the front door and illuminates the landing.

▶ IT'S NOT NECESSARILY QUANTITY but the quality and placement of light that counts. Even low-wattage lights can provide enough visibility for safe passage, especially if they are located to illuminate the walk.

▶ RESEMBLING TALL TOADSTOOLS, these lamps step down the walk and stairs as a walker would, with one at the midpoint of the walk and another opposite the stairs. Their solid, metal caps direct all the light downward, where it will be most effective.

◀ LOOKING A BIT LIKE A FLOWER on a tall, slender stem, this graceful lamp seems to grow out of the surrounding foliage. One of the advantages of this type of gooseneck lamp is that the head is adjustable; it can be swiveled to put the light exactly where it's needed.

▲ THIS SMALL FIXTURE acts as both wall decoration and light source. Since the fixture's opening points down, the light will bounce off the white wall and illuminate the stair.

◀ THE RANDOM PATTERN and varied size of these irregular flagstones create a distinctive, rustic look. Walkways constructed in this manner are typically uneven, so this kind of design is best for secondary or tertiary walks that get limited traffic.

▼ SURROUNDED BY A RIOT OF COLOR, this solid-carpet walkway moves calmly along the side of the house. The crisp white diamond tiles easily direct the path, while the red field tiles blend with their surroundings.

▲ ZIGZAGGING THROUGH an extensive array of planting beds, this walk built out of recycled bricks complements the end wall of the house. The walkway's basket-weave pattern is bordered with a sailor's course, a row of bricks installed on edge.

▲ JUST BECAUSE A WALKWAY CURVES doesn't mean the pattern of its stones must curve too. The edges of these square and rectangular flagstones were cut to the shape of the arc.

◄ THESE PRECAST CONCRETE FLAGSTONES were washed after the concrete had partially hardened, exposing the stone aggregate below the surface. Set diagonally and stitched together with ribbons of grass, they make an inviting walkway.

LOOSE-FILL WALKWAYS

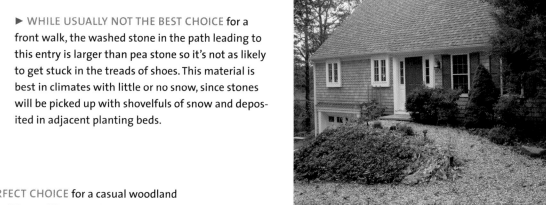

▶ WHILE USUALLY NOT THE BEST CHOICE for a front walk, the washed stone in the path leading to this entry is larger than pea stone so it's not as likely to get stuck in the treads of shoes. This material is best in climates with little or no snow, since stones will be picked up with shovelfuls of snow and deposited in adjacent planting beds.

▼ PEA STONE IS A PERFECT CHOICE for a casual woodland path. However, as with all loose-fill materials, unless pea stone is installed over a weed-blocking landscaping fabric, weeding will be a regular chore.

◄ THIS RED MULCH provides a bold background for an equally bold planting scheme. Some mulch, such as cedar, hemlock, or pine, is naturally red, but colorants are sometimes added to create really deep, rich shades.

▲ HERE, A SECONDARY PATH parallels the primary walkway, which curves crisply toward the front of the house. A more leisurely tone is set by the casual loose-fill material and imprecise edges, as opposed to its purposeful neighbor.

▲ WHILE THIS PEA-STONE and flagstone path has some tonal variation, the overall color feel complements the home's buff-colored façade.

▼ TRAVERSING A LOW HILL, this walk is actually part path and part stair. At regular intervals the sloping walk is interrupted by a single riser. Because the steps allow height to be gained over a shorter distance, the surface of the walk can be built to a shallower, safer pitch.

▲ WALKS HAVE A GREATER SENSE OF PLACE when their edges are clearly defined or when they move along a distinct boundary. One technique is to locate a walkway directly adjacent to a landscape feature, as demonstrated here.

► A NEATLY TRIMMED HEDGE forms an obvious boundary for this pea-stone walk, which, in spite of being made from an informal material, has a decidedly formal feel. And even though the hedge moves in and out, the overall impression is that of a straight path.

STEPPING-STONE PATHS

◄ IT DOESN'T MATTER that this path is nearly swallowed up by the profusion of hostas that border it. Sometimes it's just as important to experience the plantings as it is to get from one end of the path to the other.

► DESIGNED TO ENCOURAGE A SLOW PACE, this stepping-stone path leads you through a bountiful garden, inviting you to smell the flowers. Pretty and sweet-smelling plants, such as creeping thyme or oregano, grow well in joints and are hardy enough to take foot traffic.

► THE STONES IN THIS DECIDEDLY CAUSAL PATH are an effective guide for travelers through the picturesque setting. The stones are particularly useful when the surrounding area is soggy; wood chips or mulch would have provided the same casual feel but would have stayed wet longer.

◄ NO DOUBT ABOUT WHICH IS THE PRIMARY and which is the secondary walkway to this home. Where the two meet, the entrance to the stepping-stone path is clearly marked by the plantings on the left and the arrangement of rocks to the right.

▼ THE STEPPING STONES for this path are actually brick pads laid in a herringbone pattern. The design offsets each successive pad slightly so that the walker approaches the destination diagonally, not straight on.

▲ A GOOD EXAMPLE OF PATH HIERARCHY, the much smaller, tertiary stepping-stone path is made from the same material as the primary walk, but has a very different feel. A visitor standing near the front door is certain to be intrigued by what's around the corner in the sunlight.

Stepping-Stone Path

INSTALLING A STEPPING-STONE PATH is pretty easy for even the most novice do-it-yourselfer. Since this kind of path is casual by nature, you don't need to focus too much on the design. Instead, let the stones themselves—their shape, texture, and color—be the main design element.

STEP 1: First lay out the location of the path with rope, chalk, or powdered lime, then arrange the stones along the length of the path. Measure a walking stride that is comfortable for you, probably somewhere between 20 in. and 26 in., and set the distance between the center of each stone equal to that distance (24 in. in the illustration).

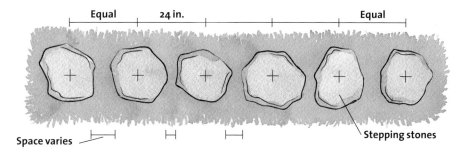

Equal   24 in.   Equal

Space varies

Stepping stones

STEP 2: Remove the stones, putting them off to the side, so you can excavate the dirt from the length of the path. Even though you could dig out an area just an inch or two larger than the stones, clearing the entire path gives you some flexibility and will probably make installing the stones easier. Excavate to a depth that will accommodate a bed of gravel between 3 in. and 6 in. deep (the exact depth of excavation depends on the area of the country you live in and your type of soil).

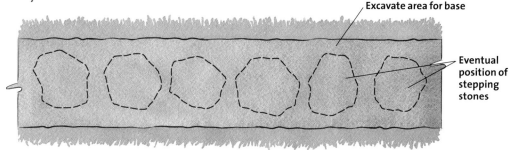

Excavate area for base

Eventual position of stepping stones

STEP 3: Now, fill the excavated area with gravel, compacting it every couple of inches; stop when the level of the gravel is below the ground's surface a distance equal to the thickness of the stones. One by one, install the stones into the gravel, wiggling them and tapping them with a heavy rubber mallet.

STEP 4: After all of the stones have been installed, fill the joints with soil and plant them with grass or low-growing plants.

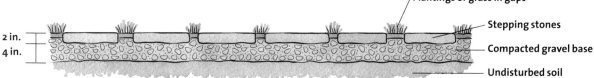

Plantings or grass in gaps

Stepping stones

2 in.
4 in.

Compacted gravel base

Undisturbed soil

MIXED-MATERIAL WALKWAYS

► CONCRETE IS A MIXTURE OF, among other things, cement and stone aggregate, but this path takes the stone part to the extreme. With the aggregate dominating, the path appears to be a river of stone.

▼ THIS WALKWAY BORROWS from an artistic photographic technique where the main subject bleeds off the edge of the paper. Instead of forming a complete pattern, some of the inset pavers are cropped by the lawn.

▲ AT FIRST GLANCE it looks as if this is simply a stepping-stone path. But with the pea stone installed level with the top of the stones, the entire width of the walk can be used. The pattern of flagstone diamonds is thus an inset design in the walkway.

▼ THE ALTERNATING SQUARE TILES and squares of grass make this walk to the side door unusual and, in this application, functional. Given the differences in how these two materials feel underfoot, this treatment shouldn't be used for a primary walk to the front door.

Filling the Joints

▲ SMALL, SIMPLE TOUCHES demonstrate thoughtful caring. As you plan your walkway, be on the lookout for ways to inject your personality by incorporating items you find unique, interesting, or that have special meaning to you.

▲ EVEN THE TIGHTEST SPACES can support plant life. Most nurseries and garden centers sell a variety of plants that will happily grow between walkway cracks and joints and that can stand up to moderate foot traffic.

▶ IT APPEARS THAT AS MUCH THOUGHT went into the gap-fillers here as the entire walk. Not only does the color of the blue stones match the adjacent plant perfectly, but the color of the concrete into which the stones are imbedded mimics the color of the plants' outermost leaves.

▲ RED BRICK AND GREEN PLANTS just seem to have an affinity for each other, but not all bricks are red. This walk has a number of bluish-gray types, which, whether by choice or by chance, are a nice complement to tiny blue flowers.

◄ THIS PATH INCORPORATES IRREGULAR FLAGSTONES and washed stone of similar tones. Even though the joints are relatively wide, they blend the two materials together and enhance the solid-carpet effect.

◄ DETAILS SUCH AS THESE INSET GRANITE PAVERS enliven and focus attention on walkways. Depending on the type of material used, you might be able to wait until the walkway is actually being constructed for inspiration to strike, or details may have to be planned ahead.

▼ THE CURVE, EVEN THOUGH IT IS SLIGHT, helps this short, simple path blend nicely with the surroundings, and allows walkers to move easily from one part of the landscape to another.

▲ LEADING TO A SMALL ENTRY PATIO, these very large flagstones of cast-in-place concrete appear to float in a sea of washed stone.

▲ A SERIES OF GENTLE CURVES seems to establish a walking rhythm, as demonstrated by this pea-stone path. Wide enough for two abreast, it's perfect for a leisurely, arm-in-arm stroll in the late afternoon.

MATERIALS IN DETAIL

Natural Building Materials

You don't always have to go to the lumberyard or home center to find building materials. Instead, take a walk through the woods to get a sense of how Mother Nature designs. Short lengths of rough saplings are used to construct this rustic arch and rail fence.

PAVER PATTERNS

► THE SQUARE PAVERS
here not only form the border
of the primary walkway but also
signal the connection with the
smaller, secondary path. They
also make a smooth transition
between the diagonally laid pavers of the larger walk and the
stacked pattern of the smaller.

◄ ALTHOUGH THERE ARE a number of
standard installation patterns typically
used for pavers, the possibilities are
really only limited by your imagination.
This walkway is a case in point. Some of
the brick pavers are installed on edge
and parallel with the length of the path
while others are face up and perpendicular. The extra wide spaces between
the pavers complete the pattern.

►CREATING A RHYTHM ALL THEIR
OWN are tangential circles laid out
in this paver walkway. In a surpris-
ing design tactic, the varying width
of the walk cuts off portions of each
circle.

▲ THE MORTARED JOINTS of this solid-carpet walkway hold the composition together. The two strips of blue pebbles are sandwiched between diagonally laid tile pavers and brick soldier pavers (installed perpendicularly to the length of a walk).

▲ TWO CLASSIC PAVER PATTERNS— the basket weave and running bond—are combined here with pleasing results. The running-bond portion of the walkway, which suggests a different travel direction, is made from different bricks than the basket-weave section and has mortared joints to emphasize the differences between the two.

Gates as Transitional Markers

▼ INSTALLING A GATE in conjunction with an arch is a classic approach. The arch not only creates a frame in which to display the gate, but it also provides the supporting posts, making the structure fairly sturdy.

▶ CLEARLY NOT INTENDED FOR PRIVACY, this round-top gate made from large wood dowels interrupts the picket fence and marks the way into the entry courtyard. A nice touch, when possible, is to install a gate using hardware that permits the gate to be opened by either pushing or pulling.

▲ GATES CAN DIVIDE the inside from the outside and, when installed in conjunction with a walkway, provide the clearest possible transitional marker, often indicating when someone is moving from the public domain into a more private realm.

▲ CAST AND WROUGHT IRON GATES have a timeless quality. To eliminate much of the maintenance associated with iron and steel—it has to be painted from time to time—gates and fences made from aluminum can be used instead.

◄ THE PLAYFUL CURVED TOP and whimsical sun cutout are an appropriate match for this informal path. Gates made from solid wood tend to be heavy and should be securely held by posts installed deep in the ground.

Steps

ALTHOUGH WALKWAYS GET TOP BILLING, steps have an indispensable part to play. Without them, negotiating slopes and differences in terrain would be difficult, if not impossible. While ramps do offer a barrier-free path, they require a relatively large amount of space and when they are wet or snow-covered, ramps can be slippery. Steps are space-efficient and, if properly designed, a safe way to move vertically through the landscape.

Steps can be categorized by their method of construction—mortared, dry laid, infill tread, one piece, and riser only. But certain types of steps are generally considered to be formal and others informal based on their style rather than the way they're built. When determining what type to build in your landscape, take into account the style of your home, how the steps are going to be used, and the character of the walkway of which they'll be a part.

▲ THERE'S NOTHING QUITE AS WELCOMING as a wide, low set of steps, as these semicircular steps clearly demonstrate. Although they take up a lot of space, the curve focuses attention on the front entry and allows people to approach or leave from several directions.

▶ IN ADDITION TO THE WIDE VARIETY of concrete pavers that are available, manufacturers also produce pieces for constructing steps and walls. For a coordinated look, choose the same style and color for pavers, steps, and walls.

▲ THE SAME THIN IRREGULAR FLAGSTONES used for the path are mortared together to build this short flight of steps. Squeezed between two rock outcroppings, the stones that make up the risers are multicolored; the effect resembles sunlight shining on the angled faces of the boulders.

◄ THESE ONE-PIECE STEPS seem to be part of the stone wall. In fact, if it wasn't for the paver walk leading up to them, they might almost disappear. Here, the juxtaposition of the rough and finished is both functional and aesthetically pleasing.

MORTARED STEPS

▲ IN A NOD TO THE TILE ROOF and light-colored stucco wall, these steps are made with red risers and treads that are the same color as the house. One way that exterior steps differ from their interior cousins is that exterior treads can, if space and the grade allows, be made very deep. The first two steps shown here probably require two strides to cover.

◄ LARGE WALKWAY FLAGSTONES, with their bold white mortar joints, project over the riser, forming the top step. The joints are alternated from one side to the other, avoiding a boring stacked look.

▲ WITHOUT A SAFE, well-constructed flight of stairs, accessing this sunken patio would be difficult. Unlike some outdoor steps, each riser formed by the wooden timbers is identical to the next, through the entire run. The predictable dimensions make negotiating these steps as easy as walking down an interior stair.

◄ TREADS THAT OVERHANG the risers below make walking on steps easier, providing a slightly wider tread surface. Another design technique is to slope the riser back from the top to the bottom.

▲ THESE STEPS INSTANTLY WELCOME guests to the front door, thanks to the wide bottom. The entire stairway would have felt very confining if these steps didn't flair at their base.

◄ PRIM AND PROPER best describes these steps, which cut through the retaining wall and are constructed with the same paving brick as the walkway. As with motared walkways, to avoid the ravages of the freeze/thaw cycle in colder areas of the country, mortared steps must be constructed on a proper gravel or washed-stone base.

► ONE WAY FOR YOUR STEPS to make a strong visual statement is to use highly contrasting materials or colors for the treads and risers. Using darker colors for the treads and lighter shades for the risers, like these, make the treads appear to float above the risers.

▼ THERE'S A LOT GOING ON in this set of steps. Mortar made it possible to construct the risers out of lots of small stones, while the treads are made of a single bluestone flagstone, quieting the effect of the risers. The walkway is interrupted by a square brick landing, inset with bluestone, which encourages folks to pause before ascending a second flight of steps.

DRY-LAID STEPS

▶ THESE DRY-LAID STEPS are carefully calculated to follow the long slope of the hill; the layout helps alleviate the need for a retaining wall to hold back the earth at the ends of the treads.

▼ ALTHOUGH STEPS WEREN'T NEEDED to traverse this low hill, they separate the lawn from the small patio and create a bit of ceremony for those who are leaving the lawn to settle down in the love seat.

◄ TRANSITION ZONES are important to delineate separate spaces in a landscape. These steps, assisted by stately stone columns, clearly signify the separation between the patio and walkway. The effect is enhanced by the horizontal line of the steps, which halts the walkway's running-bond pavers.

▲ CUT INTO THE FACE OF THE SLOPE, a line of very rough, large stones acts as a low retaining wall. The stones give one the feeling of being in the bottom of a streambed. Together with the steps they create an air of informality that is in keeping with the surrounding plantings.

◄ ORDINARILY STAIR TREADS are oriented perpendicular to the line of travel and curve or turn to change direction. This set of steps illustrates a different approach. Each successive step is offset slightly from the preceding one, creating a diagonal line of travel up the slope.

► FOR SAFETY REASONS, long flights of stairs should be broken up by landings, which give people an opportunity to stop their forward momentum. These steps not only incorporate a couple of landings but also change direction and thus the view.

▼ BUILDING STEPS IN THE LANDSCAPE provides lots of opportunities to break away from the stereotypical stairway. These dry-laid steps are part stair, part walkway. Loose-fill material marks the path, while a stepping stone placed just before each riser indicates that a step is coming.

▲ THESE STONES at the side of the stair treads appear to be merely decorative. But they actually have dual function—they act as mini-retaining walls and keep the dirt off of the edge of the treads.

▲ WITH PLANTS GROWING OUT of the base of the risers and between the joints in the treads, these steps almost seem a part of the hillside. While this certainly adds character to the steps, too much of a good thing could spell trouble. Plantings should not be allowed to obscure the stairs to the point that they become dangerous.

◀ THIN STONE TREADS, such as the one-piece flagstone used in these steps, should be evenly supported by the riser stones. If not, a sharp impact may crack the treads. Also, tread overhangs should be kept to a minimum, for the same reason.

INFILL TREADS

▶ SOMEHOW ELEGANT and rustic at the same time, this set of steps seamlessly incorporates a number of features that makes them very safe. The landscaping timbers ensure a predictable riser height, while generous flagstone landings are strategically located. The metal railings that flank the individual flights provide security when needed.

▲ ALTHOUGH DEFINITELY NOT APPROPRIATE for a set of entry steps, this unusual example of infill treads certainly grabs your attention. Each tread is, for all intents and purposes, a planting bed formed by timber risers, creating the effect of steps literally cascading down the slope.

▶ WITH LUCK, steps can sometimes be constructed with stones found on site. Such is the case with the stones that edge these gardens and make up the steps.

▲ THE ENDS OF THESE LANDSCAPING TIMBERS are installed flush with the top of the slope and have treads finished with white washed stones. Since the material underneath the stone compacts over time, additional stones may have to be added to keep them even with the top of the timber. For this reason, keep some extra on hand or make sure matching stone will be available in the future.

ONE-PIECE AND RISER-ONLY STEPS

◄ CONSTRUCTING A SET OF STEPS with massive stones like these might seem a Herculean task, but it's fairly easy with a backhoe or tractor. Large stones sometimes have at least one uneven surface; the most difficult part of the installation can be leveling them by shimming them with smaller stones.

▼ USED IN PAIRS, THESE ONE-PIECE, CUT-GRANITE STEPS complement the concrete paver walkway. The tread portion of each stone has a honed finish, which is smooth but not as slippery as a polished surface. And, to emphasize the differences between tread and riser, the latter are finished with a rough-texture surface.

▲ THE SAME SIMPLE SLABS OF CONCRETE that are used for the back step and patio also make up these understated steps. Their unadorned nature is a good fit for the relatively plain face of this home's exterior.

◄ THESE STEPS APPEAR as if they were carved directly out of the face of the hill partly because of their shape and color, but also due to their position when installed. The treads are two strides deep, which encourages a slow, thoughtful gait.

▼ WITH OVERSIZED STONES and a profusion of plants jutting out from every crevice, these steps are intended to be a place to sit and enjoy the scenery, rather than a stairway to get from one place to another.

▶ DISAPPEARING INTO A PROFUSION OF PLANTS, these one-piece stone steps connect a lower patio with the front stairs. Where needed, the thinner stones are shimmed to keep the riser height more or less uniform throughout the run.

◄ WHEN WORKING WITH NATURAL STONE it's sometimes best to go with whatever nature provided. If the two stone steps that bridge this small stream had been installed with the gap oriented parallel to the banks, they wouldn't have been wide enough to make a safe crossing. But turned, the extra length of the diagonal made the difference.

▼ ROUGH MATERIALS don't have to mean rough-looking results. The thoughtful placement of these fieldstones and large stone slabs creates a relatively finished look. Of particular interest are the two stone pillars, one consisting of three stacked stones, flanking the bottom of the steps.

Walls and Step Combinations

◄ AT FIRST GLANCE, these steps might appear to be needlessly wide, but given the size of the retaining and freestanding walls that surround them, they are appropriately scaled.

▼ SUBTLETY CAN BE AN EFFECTIVE design element. Constructed from the same material, the muted gray tones of the retaining walls and one-piece steps tone down the visual weight of the stones. And although the concrete-paver patio is a similar color, the red border creates a clear separation between the patio and stonework.

▼ OPPOSITES ATTRACT, as evidenced by this stair/wall combination. Even though the materials are completely different in style and color, they combine to make a strong statement.

▲ LOOKING VERY MUCH LIKE A FLOWING RIVER, this shallow set of concrete-paver steps cascades down the slope between banks made of dry-laid stone. Even though the steps and adjacent banks are made from different materials, they are tied together by their similar size and color variations.

Resources

ADDITIONAL READING

Environmental Building News
BuildingGreen, Inc.
A monthly newsletter featuring comprehensive information on a wide range of topics related to sustainable building including energy efficiency, recycled-content materials, and indoor air quality.

Backyard Idea Book
Lee Anne White
The Taunton Press, Inc., 2005

Fine Gardening® Magazine
The Taunton Press, Inc.

Garden Deck and Landscape® Magazine
Better Homes and Gardens®

Green Building Products
BuildingGreen, Inc.

How to Build Paths, Steps, and Footbridges
Peter Jeswald
Storey® Publishing, 2005

Outside the Not So Big House
Julie Moir Messervy and
Sarah Susanka
The Taunton Press, Inc., 2006

Pool Idea Book
Lee Anne White
The Taunton Press, Inc., 2005

PROFESSIONAL ORGANIZATIONS

American Institute of
Architects®
www.aia.org
Lists AIA member architects
that specialize in residential
work

American Institute of Building
Designers®
www.aibd.org

Association of Professional
Landscape Designers®
www.apld.org

American Society of
Landscape Architects®
www.asla.org

The Brick Industry
Association
www.bia.org

Interlocking Concrete Paver
Institute®
www.icpi.org

International Play Equipment
Manufacturers Association
www.ipema.org

Master Pools Guild™
www.masterpoolsguild.com

National Pool and Spa
Institute®
http://www.nspi.co.za/

National Association of Home
Builders
www.nahb.org

National Association of the
Remodeling Industry®
www.nari.org

WEBSITES

BuildingGreen, Inc.
www.buildinggreen.com

Building Science Corp.
www.buildingscience.com

Energy Star®
www.energystar.gov

U.S. Environmental Protection
Agency
www.epa.gov

DESIGNERS SPECIALIZING IN WATER FEATURES

Allgood Outdoors
www.allgoodoutdoors.com

Aquascape Designs
www.aquascapedesigns.com

Aquatic Construction
www.aquaticconstruction.com

Backyard Watergardens, LLC
www.backyardwatergardens.com

The Fockele Garden Company
www.fockelegardencompany.com

Potomac Waterworks
www.potomacwaterworks.com

Rik Rock Architectural Water
Environments
www.rikrock.com

CAD PROGRAMS

Landscape Master Pro™
Punch! Software®
www.punchsoftware.com/

Landscape Vision Design
Landscape Vision
www.landscapeyourvisions.com/

Yardiac®.com Custom
Landscape Design
Yardiac.com
www.yardiac.com/

Credits

CHAPTER 1

p. 4: Photo © Jesse Walker Associates

p. 6: (right) Photo © Saxon Holt Photography; (left) Photo © Chipper Hatter Photography

pp. 7–8: Photos © Saxon Holt Photography

p.9: Photo © Lee Anne White Photography

p. 10: (top) Photo © Randy O'Rourke; (bottom) Photo © Lee Anne White Photography

p. 11: (top left) Photo © Lee Anne White Photography; (top right) Photo © Randy O'Rourke; (bottom) Photo © Lisa Romerein Photography

p. 12: (right) Photo © Saxon Holt Photography; (left) Photo © Randy O'Rourke

p. 13: Photo © Saxon Holt Photography

p. 14: (top) Photo © Jesse Walker Associates; (bottom) Photo © Mark Lohman Photography

p. 15: (top) Photo © www.carolyn bates.com Photography; (bottom) Photo © Tria Giovan Photography

p. 16: (top) Photo © Jesse Walker Associates; (bottom) Photos © Lisa Romerein Photography

p. 17: (top) Photo © Lee Anne White Photography; (bottom) Photo © Linda Svendsen Photography

p. 18: Photo © Tria Giovan Photography

p. 19: Photo © www.carolynbates.com

p. 20: Photo © Lee Anne White Photography

p. 21: (top) Photo © Tim Street-Porter; (bottom) Photo © Lisa Romerein Photography

p. 22: (top) Photo © Saxon Holt Photography; (bottom) Photo © www.carolynbates.com

p. 23: (top) Photo © www.carolyn bates.com; (bottom) Photo © Lee Anne White Photography

p. 24: (top) Photo © Randy O'Rourke; (bottom) Photo © www.carolynbates.com

p. 25: Photo © Saxon Holt Photography

p. 26: (top) Photo © Steve Vierra Photography; (bottom) Photo © Lee Anne White Photography

p. 27: (top) Photo © Lisa Romerein Photography; (bottom) Photo © Jesse Walker Associates

p. 28: Photo © Jesse Walker Associates

p. 29: (left) Photo © Mark Lohman Photography; (right) Photo © Zimmerman Photography

p. 30: Photo © Lee Anne White Photography

p. 31: (top) Photo © Jesse Walker Associates; (bottom left) Photo © www.carolynbates.com; (bottom right) Photo © Lee Anne White Photography

CHAPTER 2

p. 32: Photo © Tria Giovan Photography

p. 34: (top) Photo © Lee Anne White Photography; (bottom) Photo © Mark Lohman Photography

p. 35: Photo © Saxon Holt Photography

p. 36: Photo © Tria Giovan Photography

p. 37: Photos © Mark Lohman Photography

p. 38: (top) Photo © Jesse Walker Associates; (bottom) Photo © Lee Anne White Photography

p. 39: Photos © Widstrand Photography

p. 40: (top) Photo © Lee Anne White Photography; (bottom) Photo © Steve Vierra Photography

p. 41: (top left) Photo © Lisa Romerein Photography; (top right) Photo © Lee Anne White Photography; (bottom) Photo © Saxon Holt Photography

p. 42: Photos © Saxon Holt Photography

p. 43: (top) Photo © Tim Street-Porter; (bottom) Photo © Chipper Hatter Photography

p. 44: (top) Photo © Randy O'Rourke; (bottom) Photo © Saxon Holt Photography

p. 45: Photo © Linda Svendsen Photography

p. 46: (top) Photo © Saxon Holt Photography; (bottom) Photo © Lee Anne White Photography

p. 47: (top) Photo © Lisa Romerein Photography; (bottom) Photo © Lee Anne White Photography

p. 48: Photo © Chipper Hatter Photography

p. 49: (top) Photo © Lisa Romerein Photography; (bottom) Photos © www.carolynbates.com

p. 50: (top) Photo © Randy O'Rourke; (bottom) Photos © Chipper Hatter Photography

p. 51: (top) Photo © Tim Street-Porter; (bottom) Photos © Mark Lohman

p. 52: (top) Photo © Jesse Walker Associates; (bottom) Photo © Anne Gummerson Photography

p. 53: (top) Photo © Mark Lohman Photography; (bottom) Photo © Zimmerman Photography

p. 54: (top) Photo © Mark Lohman Photography; (bottom) Photo © Saxon Holt Photography

p. 55: (top) Photo © Lisa Romerein Photography; (bottom) Photo © Tim Street-Porter

p. 57: Photos © Lisa Romerein Photography

p. 58: (top left) Photo © Anne Gummerson Photography; (top right) Photo © Lisa Romerein Photography; (bottom) Photo © Lee Anne White Photography

p. 59: Photo © Lisa Romerein Photography

p. 60: (top left) Photo © Jesse Walker Associates; (top right) Photo © Mark Lohman; (bottom) Photo © Widstrand Photography

p. 61: (top) Photo © Lee Anne White Photography; (bottom) Photo © Widstrand Photography

CHAPTER 3

p. 62: Photo © Saxon Holt Photography

p. 64: (top) Photo © Lisa Romerein Photography; (bottom) Photo © Tria Giovan Photography

p. 65: Photos © Mark Lohman Photography

p. 66: (top left) Photo © Mark Lohman Photography; (top right) Photo © Chipper Hatter Photography; (bottom) Photo © Tim Street-Porter

p. 67: (left) Photo © Mark Lohman Photography; (right) Photo © Lee Anne White Photography

p. 68: (top) Photo © Lee Anne White Photography; (bottom) Photo © Jesse Walker Associates

p. 69: Photo © Lee Anne White Photography

p. 70: (top) Photo © Anne Gummerson Photography; (bottom left) Photo © Lee Anne White Photography; (bottom right) Photo © Saxon Holt Photography

p. 71: (top) Photo © Linda Svendsen Photography; (bottom) Photo © Lee Anne White Photography

p. 72: Photos © Lee Anne White Photography

p. 73: (top and bottom left) Photos © Saxon Holt Photography; (bottom right) Photo © Mark Lohman Photography

p. 74: Photo © Tria Giovan Photography

p. 75: (top left and bottom) Photos © Saxon Holt Photography; (top right) Photo © Chipper Hatter Photography

p. 76: (left) Photo © Saxon Holt Photography; (right) Photo © Jesse Walker Associates

p. 77: (top left and bottom) Photos © Saxon Holt Photography; (top right) Photo © www.carolynbates.com

p. 79: Photo © Saxon Holt Photography

p. 80: (top left) Photo © Tim Street-Porter; (right and bottom left) Photos © Lee Anne White Photography

p. 81: Photo © Tim Street-Porter

p. 82: (top) Photo © Lee Anne White Photography; (bottom) Photo © Mark Lohman Photography

p. 83: (top) Photo © Lisa Romerein Photography; (bottom left) Photo © Lee Anne White Photography; (bottom right) Photo © Saxon Holt Photography

p. 84: (top) Photo © Lisa Romerein Photography; (bottom) Photo © Lee Anne White Photography

p. 85: (top left) Photo © Zimmerman Photography; (top right) Photo © Mark Lohman Photography; (bottom) Photo © Lee Anne White Photography

CHAPTER 4

p. 86: Photo © Tim Street-Porter

p. 88: (top) Photo © www.carolynbates.com; (bottom) Photo © Lee Anne White Photography

p. 89: (top) Photo © Lisa Romerein Photography; (bottom) Photo © Steve Vierra Photography

p. 90: (top) Photo © Mark Lohman Photography; (bottom) Photo © Lee Anne White Photography

p. 91: Photo © Lisa Romerein Photography

p. 92: Photo © Anne Gummerson Photography

p. 93: (top) Photo © Lee Anne White Photography; (bottom left) Photo © Chipper Hatter Photography; (bottom right) Photo © Randy O'Rourke

p. 94: (top left and bottom) Photos © Lee Anne White Photography; (top right) Photo © Chipper Hatter Photography; (middle) Photo © Tria Giovan Photography

p. 95: (top) Photo © Steve Vierra Photography; (bottom) Photo © Saxon Holt Photography

p. 96: (top) Photo © Lisa Romerein Photography; (bottom) Photo © Chipper Hatter Photography

p. 97: Photo © Zimmerman Photography

p. 98: (top) Photo © Lee Anne White Photography; (bottom) Photo © Tim Lee Photography

p. 99: (top) Photo © Chipper Hatter Photography; (middle) Photo © Tim Street-Porter; (bottom) Photo© Zimmerman Photography

p. 100: Photo © Chipper Hatter Photography

p. 101: (left) Photo © Chipper Hatter Photography; (right) Photo © Mark Lohman Photography

p. 102: (top) Photo © Kenneth Rice Photography; (bottom) Photo © Saxon Holt Photography

p. 104: Photo © Lee Anne White, Design: Michelle Derviss Landscapes

p. 105: Photo © Saxon Holt/ Photo-Botanic

p. 106: (top) Photo © Lee Anne White, Deisgn: Betty Ajay; (bottom) Photo © Deidra Walpole Photography, Design: Kennedy Landscape Design Associates

p. 107: (top) Photo © Lee Anne White Photography; (bottom) Photo © Saxon Holt Photography

CHAPTER 5

p. 108: Photo © Randy O'Rourke

p.110: (top) Photo: © Jesse Walker Associates; (bottom) Photo © Randy O'Rourke

p. 111: Photo © Randy O'Rourke

p. 112: Photo © Chipper Hatter Photography

p. 113: (top left) Photo © Randy O'Rourke; (top right) Photo © Zimmerman Photography; (bottom) Photo © Lee Anne White Photography

p. 114: Photos © Randy O'Rourke

p. 115: (top) Photo © Mark Lohman Photography; (middle) Photo © Lee Anne White Photography; (bottom) Photo © Randy O'Rourke

p. 116: (top right) Photo © www.carolynbates.com Photography; (bottom right) Photo © Randy O'Rourke; (left) Photo © Tria Giovan Photography

p. 117: (top) Photo © Mark Lohman Photography; (bottom) Photo © Zimmerman Photography

p. 119: (top left) Photo © Saxon Holt Photography; (top right) Photo © Mark Lohman Photography; (bottom) Photo © Chipper Hatter Photography

p. 120: (top) Photo © Chipper Hatter Photography; (bottom left) Photo © Lee Anne White Photography; (bottom right) Photo © Mark Lohman Photography

p. 121: (right) Photo © Tria Giovan Photography; (left) Photo © Mark Lohman Photography

p. 122: (top) Photo © Mark Lohman Photography; (bottom) Photo © Jesse Walker Associates

p. 123: (top) Photo © www.carolynbates.com; (bottom left) Photo © Tria Giovan Photography; (bottom right) Photo © Tim Street-Porter

p. 124: (top) Photo © Chipper Hatter Photography; (bottom) Photo © Lisa Romerein Photography

p. 125: (top) Photo © Lee Anne White Photography; (bottom) Photo © Saxon Holt Photography

p. 126: Photo © Randy O'Rourke

p. 127: (top left) Photo © Jesse Walker Associates; (top right) Photo © Philip Jensen; (bottom) Photo © Randy O'Rourke

p. 128: (top left and bottom left) Photos © Randy O'Rourke; (right) Photo © Jesse Walker Associates

p. 129: (top) Photo © Jesse Walker Associates; (bottom) Photo © Tim Street-Porter

CHAPTER 6

p. 130: Photo © Jesse Walker Associates

p. 132: Photo © Mark Samu, Samu Studios, Inc.

p. 133: (left) Photo © Saxon Holt Photography; (top) Photo © Lisa Romerein Photography; (bottom) Photo © Linda Svendsen Photography

p. 134: (top left) Photo © Randy O'Rourke; (top right) Photo © Jesse Walker Associates; (bottom left) Photo © Saxon Holt Photography; (bottom middle) Photo © Mark Samu, Samu Studios, Inc.; (bottom right) Photo © www.carolynbates.com

p. 136: (top left and bottom left) Photos © Lee Anne White Photography; (top right) Photo © Saxon Holt Photography

p. 137: Photos © Tim Street-Porter

p. 138: (left) Photo © Chipper Hatter Photography; (right) Photo © Saxon Holt Photography

p. 139: (top) Photo © Steve Vierra Photography; (bottom) Photo © www.carolynbates.com

p. 140: (top left) Photo © Lee Anne White Photography; (top right) Photo © Lisa Romerein Photography; (bottom) Photo © Tria Giovan Photography

p. 141: Photos © Lee Anne White Photography

p. 142: (left) Photo © Saxon Holt Photography; (right) Photo © Mark Lohman Photography

p. 143: (top left) Photo © Jesse Walker Associates; (top right) Photo © www.carolynbates.com; (bottom) Photo © Widstrand Photography

p. 144: (top) Photo © Randy O'Rourke; (bottom) Photo © Gary Easter Photographics

p. 145: (top) Photo © Jesse Walker Associates; (right) Photo © Lisa Romerein Photography

p. 146: Photo © Tim Street-Porter

p. 147: (top left) Photo © Lisa Romerein Photography; (top right) Photo © Lee Anne White Photography; (bottom) Photo © Jesse Walker Associates

p. 148: (top) Photo © Jesse Walker Associates; (bottom) Photo © Lee Anne White Photography

p. 149: Photo © Mark Lohman Photography

p. 150: (top) Photo © Lee Anne White Photography; (bottom left) Photo © www.carolynbates.com; (bottom right) Photo © Chipper Hatter Photography

p. 152: Photos © Lee Anne White Photography

p. 153: (left) Photo © Lee Anne White Photography; (right) Photo © Tria Giovan Photography

p. 154: (top left) Photo © Saxon Holt Photography; (top right and bottom) Photos © Lee Anne White Photography

p. 155: Photos © Lee Anne White Photography

p. 156: (top) Photo © Saxon Holt Photography; (bottom) Photo © Lee Anne White Photography

p. 157: (top left) Photo © Lisa Romerein Photography; (top right) Photo © Lee Anne White Photography; (bottom) Photo © Jesse Walker Associates

p. 158: Photos © Lee Anne White Photography

p. 159: (left and bottom right) Photos © Chipper Hatter Photography; (top right) Photo © Lee Anne White Photography

p. 160: Photos © Jesse Walker Associates

p. 161: (top left) Photo © Anne Gummerson Photography; (top right) Photo © Jesse Walker Associates; (bottom) Photo © www.carolynbates.com

p. 162: (top) Photo © Lisa Romerein Photography; (bottom) Photo © Chipper Hatter Photography

p. 163: (left) Photo © Mark Samu, Samu Studios, Inc.; (right) Photo © Saxon Holt Photography

p. 164: (top) Photo © Lisa Romerein Photography; (bottom) Photo © Lee Anne White Photography

p. 165: Photos © Saxon Holt Photography

pp. 166–167: Photos © Lee Anne White Photography

p. 168: (top) Photo © Lee Anne White Photography; (bottom) Photo © www.carolynbates.com

p. 169: (top left) Photo © Lisa Romerein Photography; (right and bottom left) Photos © Lee Anne White Photography

p. 170: (top) Photo © Lisa Romerein Photography; (bottom) Photo © Lee Anne White Photography

p. 171: (top left) Photo © www.carolynbates.com; (right and bottom left) Photos © Lee Anne White Photography

p. 172: (top right) Photo © Lee Anne White Photography; (bottom left) Photo © Tim Street-Porter; (bottom right) Photo © Saxon Holt Photography

p. 173: Photo © Lee Anne White Photography

p. 174: (top) Photo © www.carolynbates.com; (bottom) Photo © Steve Vierra Photography

p. 175: (top) Photo © Lisa Romerein Photography; (bottom) Photo © Lee Anne White Photography

p. 176: (left) Photo © Lisa Romerein Photography; (right) Photo © Lee Anne White Photography

p. 177: (top) Photo © Lee Anne White Photography; (bottom) Photo © Steve Vierra Photography

p. 178: (top) Photo © www.carolynbates.com; (bottom) Photo © Lee Anne White Photography

p. 179: (left) Photo © Chipper Hatter Photography; (right) Photo © Steve Vierra Photography

For More Great Design Ideas, Look for These and Other Taunton Press Books Wherever Books are Sold.

NEW KITCHEN IDEA BOOK
1-56158-693-5
Product #070773
$19.95 U.S./$27.95 Canada

NEW BATHROOM IDEA BOOK
1-56158-692-7
Product #070774
$19.95 U.S./$27.95 Canada

NEW KIDSPACE IDEA BOOK
1-56158-694-3
Product #070776
$19.95 U.S./$27.95 Canada

NEW BUILT-INS IDEA BOOK
1-56158-673-0
Product #070755
$19.95 U.S./$27.95 Canada

TILE IDEA BOOK
1-56158-709-5
Product #070785
$19.95 U.S./$27.95 Canada

ORGANIZING IDEA BOOK
1-56158-780-X
Product #070835
$14.95 U.S./$21.00 Canada

STONESCAPING IDEA BOOK
1-56158-763-X
Product #070824
$14.95 U.S./$21.00 Canada

OUTDOOR LIVING IDEA BOOK
1-56158-757-5
Product #070820
$19.95 U.S./$27.95 Canada

BACKYARD IDEA BOOK
1-56158-667-6
Product #070749
$19.95 U.S./$27.95 Canada

TAUNTON'S HOME STORAGE IDEA BOOK
1-56158-676-5
Product #070758
$19.95 U.S./$27.95 Canada

TAUNTON'S FAMILY HOME IDEA BOOK
1-56158-729-X
Product #070789
$19.95 U.S./$27.95 Canada

TAUNTON'S HOME WORKSPACE IDEA BOOK
ISBN 1-56158-701-X
Product #070783
$19.95 U.S./$27.95 Canada

POOL IDEA BOOK
1-56158-764-8
Product #070825
$19.95 U.S./$27.95 Canada

BABYSPACE IDEA BOOK
1-56158-799-0
Product #070857
$14.95 U.S./$21.00 Canada

DECORATING IDEA BOOK
1-56158-762-1
Product #070829
$24.95 U.S./$34.95 Canada

WINDOW TREATMENTS IDEA BOOK
1-56158-819-9
Product #070869
$19.95 U.S./$26.95 Canada

COLOR IDEA BOOK
1-56158-914-2
Product #070932
$19.95 U.S./$25.95 Canada

WATER GARDEN IDEA BOOK
1-56158-877-0
Product #070920
$19.95 U.S./$25.95 Canada